CROWD-SOURCED SYLLABUS

CROWD-SOURCED SYLLABUS
A Curriculum for Resistance

BY
LEANNE MCRAE

United Kingdom – North America – Japan – India
Malaysia – China

Emerald Publishing Limited
Howard House, Wagon Lane, Bingley BD16 1WA, UK

First edition 2021

© 2021 Leanne McRae.
Published under exclusive licence by Emerald Publishing Limited

Reprints and permissions service
Contact: permissions@emeraldinsight.com

No part of this book may be reproduced, stored in a retrieval system, transmitted in any form or by any means electronic, mechanical, photocopying, recording or otherwise without either the prior written permission of the publisher or a licence permitting restricted copying issued in the UK by The Copyright Licensing Agency and in the USA by The Copyright Clearance Center. Any opinions expressed in the chapters are those of the authors. Whilst Emerald makes every effort to ensure the quality and accuracy of its content, Emerald makes no representation implied or otherwise, as to the chapters' suitability and application and disclaims any warranties, express or implied, to their use.

British Library Cataloguing in Publication Data
A catalogue record for this book is available from the British Library

ISBN: 978-1-83867-272-0 (Print)
ISBN: 978-1-83867-271-3 (Online)
ISBN: 978-1-83867-273-7 (Epub)

INVESTOR IN PEOPLE

For Steve Redhead – a mentor and all-round excellent human being

CONTENTS

About the Author ix
Acknowledgements xi

Introduction: An Ultra-Realist Refusal 1
1. An Education in Crisis: Economics, Experts and Enlightenment 11
2. The Lads: A Rebellious Refusal of Resilience 25
3. Disintermediating the Archives: Evental Education 37
4. #FergusonSyllabus 49
5. #NewFascismSyllabus 61
6. #StandingRockSyllabus 73
7. #RapeCultureSyllabus 85
8. #SanctuarySyllabus 97
9. #BlackDisabledWomanSyllabus 111
Conclusion: Popular Provocations: #LemonadeSyllabus and #ColinKaepernickSyllabus 123

Index 133

ABOUT THE AUTHOR

Leanne McRae is an independent scholar who has spent 17 years within the higher education sector as a lecturer, course co-ordinator and tutor. She now works independently to pursue research interests spanning cultural studies, critical disability studies, popular cultural studies, criminology, physical cultural studies, surveillance, and deviant leisure. Her first book published by Emerald in 2018 is entitled *Terror, Leisure and Consumption: Spaces for Harm in a Post-Crash Era*. Leanne is currently working on her third book with Tara Brabazon and Steve Redhead entitled *Moving on Up: Physical Cultural Studies*. A fourth book is also in production entitled *Secrecy, Surveillance and the State: Defining Crime, Managing Harm, and Protecting Privacy* for Rowman & Littlefield.

ACKNOWLEDGEMENTS

This book was difficult to write, coming together through trying times. My sincere thanks for helping me through this experience must go firstly to Tara Brabazon who instilled in me a rigorous approach to both teaching and scholarship. My interest in education and digitisation has been shaped by her influence. I am incredibly grateful to Katie Ellis for her patience and support. I could not ask for a better boss. I am indebted to Antonio Cerrone for his tolerance of my regular disappearance upstairs to work. I must also acknowledge Steve Hall whose indulgence of an intellectual tourist dabbling in his field was borne with good humour and has unfurled new pathways for investigation. Many thanks also to Emerald for their enduring forbearance.

Introduction

AN ULTRA-REALIST REFUSAL

> *It is power itself that has to be abolished – and not just in the refusal* to be dominated, *which is the essence of all traditional struggles, but equally and as violently in the refusal* to dominate.[1]

This book is about the double refusal. It contemplates the interventions, resistances and critical literacies needed to conjure the conditions where a double refusal is possible in everyday life. This stands slightly askew to how the double refusal is conventionally understood as not simply a rejection of power by those dominated, but by those who might wield power as well. The rise of right-wing leaders who appear confused about leadership and the responsibilities it entails, namely Boris Johnson in the United Kingdom, Donald Trump in the United States and Scott Morrison in Australia, characterises the refusal to dominate through incompetence, ignorance and apathy. It is this latter configuration that is skewed in this book. For too long scholarly emphasis has been focussed on the refusal to be dominated (resistance) without considering what it means to refuse to dominate. That space is now often occupied with critiques of the refusal to *lead*. This book argues that the current pathways presented through education, toward social mobility and into critical thinking as socially transformative and personally emancipatory function covertly as an initiation into domination. The crowd-sourced syllabus interrupts and rejects this outcome for education, learning and literacy.

Education is 'presented as an unequivocally benevolent force'[2] for social and personal development. How and what is taught in schools and at university is defined by dominant tropes that leverage the value in knowledge to a time and place. Contemporary debates about crisis in education are bolstered by concerns about producing viable and resilient work-ready graduates. Education for employment dominates this thinking. The neoliberal subject is advanced and employment is championed as the endgame of education. Knowledge is another commodity to be sold. The commodification of the flexible, adaptive thinker dovetails into the caches of critical thinking repertoires. Value in critical thinking as an end in itself is assigned to elitist and idle strategies of leisured learning. The purpose of resilience in emphasising personal responsibility amplifies cultures of work as the space in which the benevolence of education is recognised and realised.

The argument in this book leverages the concepts of The Event, the everyday real and the refusal to trouble these expectations of education. The relationships between information, knowledge and expertise re-align in the crowd-sourced or hashtag syllabus to navigate the gaping absences in education unable to deal with moments of eruption within accelerated capitalism. Claustropolitan times require radical thinking.[3] Such skills are devalued in an education focussed on preparing students for work. Critical thinking is increasingly in service of employment priorities, and the radical or disobedient is codified as deviant, dangerous and even disastrous. This book affirms the importance of radical thinking and dangerous literacies in difficult times. Educational repertoires which cultivate skills in the professional as well as the personal are shrinking to profitable pathways. The argument in this book aims to reopen the dialogue between information, the self and society by reinserting the complex values of knowledge and expertise within everyday repertoires of knowing. The significance of the everyday real as the space where struggles over meanings are performed is centralised. An interrogation of this space is affirmed as essential to the interruption of claustropolitan consciousness. It is the crowd-sourced syllabus that permits this investigation. Within this space radical thinking makes way for an educated hope and the double refusal.

Paul Virilio asserts that we now 'live in the instant of the real, which is the acceleration of reality that completely effaces history'.[4] This effacement is written in the ways in which 'the real' has been disconnected from everyday sense-making. Steve Hall and Simon Winlow contextualise the importance of this erasure and argue that it impoverishes intellectual endeavour by limiting the perspectives, presumptions and perceptions that generate meaning. They argue for intellectual disobedience.

> *What we need now is a new academic and political realism that looks coldly at the world and its problems, sizing them up carefully, drawing on the best and most up-to-date empirical data, before intervening with a view to setting us on a new course.*[5]

The tools currently available to conceptualise, render and compose the 'real' are inadequate. They argue for an 'ultra-realist' approach which destabilises 'grand theories'[6] that mask an 'ability to engage with and represent the real world'.[7] It is a rejection of 'resistance', asserting that this struggle accommodates rather than overturns existing power structures by replacing '"privileged" perspectives with "suppressed knowledges"'.[8] The ultra-realist project requires a 'rethinking' of the principles and paradigms that determine how we make sense of the everyday. This critical 'rethinking' takes established knowledges to task and theorises new approaches.

> *This act of rethinking means that one should countenance the possibility that orthodox positions are not just wrong, but may be actual impediments to understanding, or ideological constructions produced to 'cover up' reality.*[9]

This book utilises the 'ultra-realist' ethos as the propulsion to deploy a 'rethinking' of education, social mobility, resistance, digitisation, modernity and the neoliberal subject. This rethinking project spotlights the claustropolitan networking of 'accelerated culture, foreclosure and reproletarianisation'[10] that sustains the decaying and archaic principles of modernity that persist despite the myriad of 'posts'[11] punctuating the post-War, post-Crash period. The endurance of capitalism and the corroding of consciousness that sustains it is at the interface of a crisis in the real. This 'interplay between grand-scale socio-historical transformations and the ways in which they structure and mould everyday life as the material and symbolic foundations for aspirations, beliefs, desires, norms, values and all manner of sensibilities'[12] is increasingly opaque due to its complexity and the competing interests that drown the literacies and resources available to understand these intersections. The crowd-sourced syllabus re-opens the possibilities for intervention and re-imagining the variety of potentialities in the real.

Virilio argues that 'history is accidental now, instantaneous, it cancels out … the tripartite division of past, present, and future'.[13] In this context collapse, we are increasingly affronted and confronted with eruptions and destabilisation within the social where meanings spill out and beyond the normalising interfaces that limit and contain knowledge. These interruptions cascade on Twitter as a space for accelerated communication where disruption and disagreement are normalised. Appropriately called 'bursty dynamics'[14] the uneven, eruptive nature of Twitter mirrors the emergence of discontinuity in the real. It becomes the instrument for the accidental and instantaneous real to be deployed, 'hashed-out' and re-interpreted.

As the dominant folksonomy on Twitter, the hashtag permits peculiar networking of knowledge. A hashtag is not just a keyword. Its original operation in telephony was

> ...to confirm the entry of telephone numbers, account numbers or credit card numbers – its purpose, that is, was to signal the end of meaningful data and issue a command to send this information.[15]

A hashtag simultaneously opens and closes potentialities within the digitised space, making its 'bursty' nature an ideal tool for exchange of information, experiences and ideas in accelerated interactions. This simultaneous opening and closing, possibility and contention enables the space for a double refusal. The crowd-sourced syllabus is an indexing of possibilities – a simultaneity of the real and a mobile memory archive of potential ways of being, knowing and understanding. It maps an evolving, living, changing, colliding and reforming real as it projects into the past, within the present and for the future. Knowledge is dislodged from official educational oeuvres and the hashtag permits collision of possibilities.

The first crowd-sourced syllabus was created by Marcia Chatelain following the fatal police shooting of Michael Brown Jr., in Ferguson, Missouri, in 2014. Chatelain leveraged her Twitter followers to gather resources to help teach the tragedy in her classroom. This call for resources indicates that contemporary educational repertoires were inadequate to her teaching needs. The eruption caused by Michael Brown Jr.'s murder provided a fulcrum for negotiations over 'the real'. Her initiative precipitated multiple imitators that leveraged the utility of the hashtag to curate and cultivate contested knowledges into a radical rethink of the real. These syllabi draw on the expertise of theorists, academics, teachers, activists, journalists and others who contribute articles, photographs, oral histories, polemics and films to readings lists and resource archives. Their contributions are submitted and distributed using the # symbol. Users can search Twitter to find these contributions and offer their own. The deployment of the hashtag in this manner is different to the activist tags that circulate to 'rapidly amass large numbers of protesters with a common goal'[16] as seen in the Arab Spring or Occupy Wall Street. The outcome of the syllabus is not pre-configured; rethinking rather than resistance is the objective. The syllabi do not have key graduate outcomes, assessments or assigned credit. They are askew from the criteria of standardised education and not akin to MOOCs or short courses aimed at lifelong learners leveraging freemium models of internet commerce to sell knowledge. The crowd-sourced syllabus unfurls the present by leveraging the past, pre- and post-educational repertoires, and precarious knowledges in a dialogue deploying the tropes of deep thinking to reassert knowing as radical social practice. These syllabi conjure pasts, moments and memories that have been forgotten, hidden, masked and deprioritised in the contemporary educational milieu. Within these complexities alternatives to current consciousness are conjured. Refusal is realised, situated and deployed. Its nuance situates where the potential of the refusal to be dominated is visualised as well as the refusal to dominate.

Jon Savage's maxim that '[h]istory is made by those who say "No"'[17] reveals the productivities of refusing. This is not about being 'against', but how one might refuse to dominate as an act of consciousness as well as praxis. Henry Giroux and Peter McLaren express concern about defeatism in the refusal.[18] The argument in this book affirms the importance of the hesitation and the critical space the refusal enables. Educated hope is in place of nihilism and presents possibilities for a radical re-imagination of knowledge and the efficacy of expertise. Instead of polarising education – either as a neoliberal tool for marginalising students into work-ready drones for a crisis-laden economy, or as politicised pedagogues ready to enact critical thinking and radical learning to resist and rebel – educated hope activates literacies of transformation.

> *the possibility for transforming hope and politics into an ethical space and public act that confronts the flow of everyday experience and the weight of social suffering with the force of individual and collective resistance and the unending project of democratic social transformation.*[19]

Educated hope is a form of militant optimism that recodifies how we are 'informed about the limits of the present'[20] so that radical praxis can be enabled. The crowd-sourced syllabus fuses politics and hope erupting out of the moment or 'the event' where meanings become destabilised. In offering space for refusals the hashtag is the conduit through which this eruption is visualised and rendered via 'the real'. The crowd-scoured syllabus operationalises the potential for double refusal by conjuring contested and contestable ways of knowing, being and understanding in curated exchanges.

This book utilises the crowd-sourced syllabi to rethink the relationships to knowledge, hope, refusal and radical change. The chapters that follow move through these potentials, flowing and hesitating to consider the complexities that coincide to navigate the claustropolitan conditions that limit and restrain unpopular modes of thinking. In these spaces resistance relinquishes to the refusal. The potential for the double refusal is seductive and seditious because it presents the possibility for radical thinking and change. The syllabi are not just tools for teaching and learning. They are also a meditation on how knowledge, knowing and knower occupy discrete places within the negotiation of the everyday real. By understanding these components and how they interact, rethinking becomes possible, unhindered by claustropolitan urgencies.

Chapter 1 upsets the familiar refrain of educational crisis in the neoliberal era. Instead of treading the well-worn arguments about the decline of educational standards and the rise of the corporate university, this chapter considers the dilemmas of expertise. This chapter refuses to normalise the accusation of racism, sexism and stupidity of voters who elected Donald Trump, affirmed Brexit and side with populist movements. The assertions of ignorance when more people than ever are enrolling in education, are credentialed and have reliable access to the reams of online information on the internet and the web sit awkwardly in this debate. Literacy offers only one explanation. This chapter suggests that the reification of reactivity over reading is part of a corroding educational terrain where alternative knowledges are being struggled over.

Chapter 2 revisits Paul Willis' *Learning to Labour* to argue that the lads presented possibilities for a double refusal. The working-class lads in Willis' study have been frequently exemplified and his study lionised as an intellectual crucible demonstrating how working-class lads choose to sabotage their opportunities in life, and how educational institutions assist them in this project. Critical pedagogies that came after Willis reshaped educational landscapes by considering how pedagogy could intervene in institutional meanings. This chapter instead suggests that the lads were enacting a double refusal. The social mobility that is the desired outcome of education involves the adoption of principles of personal improvement through rational thought and civilising procedures. The lads recognised they were being asked to trade one form of domination for another. They exemplified Baudrillard's maxim that 'the masses aren't stupid enough to let representation, power and responsibility be palmed off on them'.[21] The lads embraced subversion in their schooling to create space for refusal.

Chapter 3 connects digitisation to Alain Badiou's configuration of The Event. Via an understanding of disintermediation suspicion of expertise, decline of trust and rejection of scholarship are filtered through the emergence of an edited public culture. The Event is a radical upheaval but its causes and consequences remain obscure because the meanings defy the structures that already exist to manage 'the real'. The crowd-sourced syllabus is a navigation of evental moments. Eruptions that cannot be contained within accelerated capitalism quickly appear on and through social media (Twitter) where reactions congregate and cohere. The potential evental nature of this eruption is negotiated in the creation of the crowd-sourced syllabus which draws together resources to help make sense of the eruption. The stimulation of this intellectual labour is framed by the gaps and absences within contemporary education to provide the raw materials to investigate and render the everyday 'real'. The disruption in accelerated capitalism that cannot be explained away as resistances are configured as refusals which open the possibility for a double refusal.

Chapter 4 begins the case studies that exemplify the potential for the double refusal. The #FergusonSyllabus marks the beginning of the crowd-sourced syllabus movement when Marcia Chatelain asked for fellow teachers to help build an archive that could provide the materials responsive to the context, moments and memories of violence in Ferguson as they emerged. This temporally responsive resource network was built upon radical knowledge and refusal to be uninformed.

Chapter 5 examines the #NewFascismSyllabus and interrogates the anxious precarity of this syllabus in its reaffirming of elite understandings of education and the function of knowledge. It straddles difficult terrain in assuming a critical literacy in its readers while also diversifying its resources to present a reified knowledge network for understanding terror, deviance, violence and resistance. The refusal embedded in the #NewFascismSyllabus is of lazy thinking. The merits of difficult thinking are enfolded throughout with assumptions about literacy peppering the material. Nevertheless, the syllabus also permits practicalities and praxis to inform its approaches to diversify the ways of knowing via an educated hope.

Chapter 6 examines the most detailed and diversified syllabi of the case studies with the #StandingRockSyllabus. The materials that are cohered constitute an archive of endurance and present a direct challenge to the tropes of resilience that have come to punctuate contemporary educational efficacies. The memory of the Oceti Sakowin transcends the educated resilience of neoliberal subjectivity. The protesters at Standing Rock do not deploy resistance. They activate ways of knowing and being that have endured. This is a timeless refusal of generations and an ongoing reaffirmation of connection to land and water rights as the colonial settler project consistently seeks to strip them of their ways of knowing. The presence of the double refusal is palpable and powerful.

Chapter 7 interrogates the refusal of consent. Stimulated in response to *The New York Times* exposé on Harvey Weinstein that outed him as a serial sexual predator, the #MeToo movement visualises the routine and regular exploitation of women's bodies in their everyday real. The rape culture syllabus was aggregated via the #NotOkay hashtag that asserted a clear rejection of the bodily incursions normalised in women's experiences. Consent is a site for struggle, and the syllabus coheres challenging ways of knowing gender, corporeality, violence and sexuality required for meanings to be navigated and destabilised.

Chapter 8 diverts into the sanctuary movement to question the assertion of power and its invitation into the everyday to define and shape 'the real'. Sanctuary cities and campuses in the United States are sites of struggle over the power wielded by the office of the president and Donald Trump specifically. A sanctuary campus offers an educated hope and a refusal to obey presidential directives aimed at undocumented residents and students. The power of paper to track, legitimate and assert power is affirmed but also questioned by the sanctuary campus movement via a refusal to aggregate and deploy documents identifying 'illegals' to Immigration and Customs Enforcement. These struggles are based at the heart of constitutional and presidential power, and the educational literacies that enable and visualise refusal.

The final case study coheres disability, race and gender to investigate the creation of the Black Disabled Woman Syllabus. Embodied binaries between abled and disabled constructed in Vilissa Thompson's narrative of the creation of this syllabus identify how the intellectual labour of people with disabilities remains obscured. The routine refusals that must be enacted by people with disabilities as their human rights are rewritten and denied form a site where repressed truths rise up. The disabled body is a site of contestation over what is 'real', right and true. The medical and social models for understanding and representing disability contest in these spaces. The syllabus takes the terrain of representation as critical space for rethinking, re-imagining and re-knowing disability.

This book is punctuated by the figure and fallibilities of Donald Trump. Many of the syllabi selected for study were created in response to his nomination as Republican Party candidate or his eventual election to the presidency of the United States. The role of #BlackLivesMatter in popularising resistance via social media has also formed a foundation for the interrogation of the relationships between rethinking, evental eruptions, and 'the real' in this book. As of writing, the murder of George Floyd by police in Minneapolis has resulted in widespread rioting in the United States as the coronavirus marches onward and upward of 100,000 deaths from the disease. These happenings are ripe for evental intervention. Police power and government authority is being burnt in the streets. Radical thinking is rebelling against the staid structures of the old. Educated hope reinforces the debates and discussions about violence, rebellion, social change, policing and racism. There is an arrival of intellect and a celebration of knowing. Rhetoric and evocative oratory is populating newsfeeds and archives. This is not a time of ignorance. It is a time of anger and a time of refusal. The double refusal bubbles in anticipation as the times of Trump conclude and the evental potentiality of the eruptive present manifests in crowd-sourced syllabi that reorder and reanimate ways of knowing that encircle and entreat education. The hope of radical rethinking opens possibilities for new ways of configuring power that might present pathways for a double refusal.

NOTES

1. Jean Baudrillard, *Carnival and Cannibal or the Play of Global Antagonism* (London: Seagull Books, 2010), 17–18.
2. Sam Friedman, "Habitus Clivé and the Emotional Imprint of Social Mobility," *The Sociological Review* 64, (2016): 130, https://doi.org/10.1111%2F1467-954X.12280.
3. Steve Redhead, *We Have Never Been Postmodern: Theory at the Speed of Light* (Edinburgh: Edinburgh University Press, 2011), 119.
4. Paul Virilio, "Celebration: A World of Appearances," interview by Sacha Goldman, *Cultural Politics* 8, no. 1, (2012): 62, https://doi.org/10.1215/17432197-1571985.
5. Simon Winlow and Steve Hall, "Shock and Awe: On Progressive Minimalism and retreatism and the new ultra-realism," *Critical Criminology* 27, (2019): 25 https://doi.org/10.1007/s10612-019-09431-1.
6. Steve Hall and Simon Winlow, "Ultra-realism," in *Routledge Handbook of Critical Criminology*, eds. Walter S. Dekeseredy and Molly Dragiewicz (London: Routledge, 2018), 44.
7. Hall and Winlow, "Ultra-realism," 44.
8. Hall and Winlow, "Ultra-realism," 44.
9. Steve Hall and Simon Winlow, "Introduction: The Need for New Directions in Criminological Theory," in *New Directions in Criminological Theory*, eds. Steve Hall and Simon Winlow (London: Routledge, 2012), 7.
10. Steve Redhead, *Theoretical Times* (Bingley: Emerald, 2018), 12.
11. Redhead, *We Have Never Been Postmodern*, 2.
12. Mark Horsley, Justin Kotzé, and Steve Hall, "The Maintenance of Orderly Disorder: Modernity, Markets and the Pseudo-Pacification Process," *Journal of European History of Law* 6, no. 1, (2015): 14 http://insight.cumbria.ac.uk/id/eprint/1949/1/Horsley_TheMaintenanceOfOrderly.pdf.
13. Paul Virilio interview by Sacha Goldman: 62.
14. Seth Meyers and Jure Leskovec, "The Bursty Dynamics of the Twitter Information Network," *WWW'14*, April 7–11, 2014, http://dx.doi.org/10.1145/2566486.2568043.
15. Andreas Bernard, *Theory of the Hashtag* (Cambridge: Polity Press, 2018), 24.
16. Zeynep Turfekci, *Twitter and Tear Gas: The Power and Fragility of Networked Protest* (New Haven: Yale University Press, 2017), xxiii.
17. Jon Savage, *England's Dreaming: Anarchy, Sex Pistols, Punk Rock and Beyond* (New York: St. Martin's Press, 1992), 541.
18. Henry Giroux and Peter McLaren, "Teacher Education as Counterpublic Sphere: Radical Pedagogy as a Form of Cultural Politics," *Philosophy and Social Criticism* 12, no. 1, (1987): 55.
19. Henry Giroux, "Educated Hope in an Age of Privatized Visions," *Cultural Studies, Critical Methodologies* 2, no. 1, (2002): 102.
20. Giroux, "Educated Hope in an Age of Privatized Visions," 102.
21. Jean Baudrillard, *The Divine Left: A Chronicle of the Years 1977– 1984*, trans. David L. Sweet (Los Angeles: Semiotext(e), 2014), 52.

1

AN EDUCATION IN CRISIS: ECONOMICS, EXPERTS AND ENLIGHTENMENT

The new undergraduate programme at the University of Sydney evidently did not meet even these modest expectations of the students. The core components, Economics I and Economics II, were seen by many of them as overly theoretical, too mathematical, poorly taught and oriented towards one particular set of economic doctrines to the detriment of a fuller understanding of the real world. Too many unrealistic assumptions seemed to be made, assumptions that required them to suspend disbelief while learning the proffered theories. First-year core microeconomics lectures by Warren Hogan and second-year macroeconomics lectures by Colin Simkin were particular focal points for these criticisms.[1]

Our economics education has raised one paradigm, often referred to as neoclassical economics, to the sole object of study. Alternative perspectives have been marginalised. This stifles innovation, damages creativity and suppresses constructive criticisms that are so vital for economic understanding. Furthermore, the study of ethics, politics and history are almost completely absent from the syllabus. We propose that economics cannot be understood with all these aspects excluded; the discipline must be redefined.[2]

Two quotes invoke events quaking economics education in opposing hemispheres 40 years apart. The first comes from Gavan Butler, Evan Jones and Frank Stilwell's 2009 book *Political Economy Now!* mapping the crises in economics education at the University of Sydney which examines the shake-up of the economics discipline at the university upon the appointment of mainstream economists Warren Hogan and Colin Simkin to the department in

1968. The second is from the Post-Crash Economics Society formed at the University of Manchester in 2012 following the Global Financial Crisis of 2008 in open resistance to an economics curriculum the students claim 'fails to meet the University's own standards for an undergraduate degree'.[3] In both circumstances, the teaching of economics is a battleground for questioning what comprises a relevant and timely education.[4]

These debates reflect an ongoing tumult over the role of education within society. The discussion about a relevant economics education is now profoundly about how and what is taken up as a rigorous approach to knowing and understanding a social framework. It is an epicentre of crisis in expertise where the ascendancy of economics knowledge as an organising foundation for society has profound impacts upon what is understood as truthful and tangible in 'the real' of everyday life. Accelerated capitalism normalises 'neoliberal economisation'[5] that inserts economics-based thinking at all levels of governance, institutional organisation and domestic realities. There can be little doubt that the structure and type of economics education that gained sway in Australia in the 1970s and in the United Kingdom, leading up to the Global Financial Crisis, has significantly framed not only what and how economists advise policy makers, report in the media and define as acceptable market management but also how ordinary people understand the workings of the nation-state. In these circumstances, 'the overall trend of reducing politics to economics is clear'.[6] Monetary management is the defining trope of a successful democracy in its advancement of the well-being of its citizens. What economists are being trained in is imperative. The knowledges they advance is crucial to understanding of how everyday realities are being crafted and understood, rejected and reinterpreted.

Over the course of the twentieth century, from a position of relative marginality,[7] economists have edged their way into holding the essential expertise to manage, shape and frame political and social institutions. In the United Kingdom, there are now 'twice as many economists employed in the civil service as there are other social researchers'.[8] These numbers have been motivated by the increasing obscuring and technicalising of economics knowledge to generate 'more rigorous and scientific'[9] grounding for the discipline. The scientisation of economics serves to distance it from its social sciences origin in order to harden its study and application. The ultimate outcome has 'little room for the citizen in economic discussions and decision-making, since economic issues are discussed in a language few can engage with and in places few have access to'.[10] Political decisions are now almost entirely operationalised by complex economic equations.

If neoliberal political systems need an expert rationale for their activities, neoclassical economics normally provides it. So, if you want to cut taxes for the rich and for big corporations, there is the Laffer curve and supply-side economics. If you wish to defend cuts to government spending, there is the Rahn curve... Many of these theories and ideas lack real empirical evidence to support them, or they rely on nonsensical logic. All too often, they are built on abstract models and require the exclusion of real-world factors to work. In several cases, they are really just ideologies masquerading as objective realities... None of this, however, stops elites overtly referring to them to substantiate their decisions as and when required.[11]

Political decisions are regulated and monitored by obscurely credentialed economists, whose educational foundations are increasingly critiqued. Analysts assert students are being 'surrounded by a series of diagrammatical and mathematical models that frame economic issues as purely mechanical problems with clear right-or-wrong answers'[12] without adequate understanding of social context and the complexities of human desire, subjectivities and interpersonal politics. This narrows the economics field to neoclassical approaches that limit independent research and abstract thinking. These claims are supported by quantitative research into journal citations in the 1990s which found 'merely 10 percent of the citations that five first-tier economics journals made between 1995 and 1997 are interdisciplinary and the majority of these go to finance'.[13] Such narrowness in citation trends demonstrates a tendency towards intellectual closure. This is cause for concern when economics is used as a basis for decision-making across the social, cultural and political spectrum and holds sway in public discourse, governance and policy-making. The struggles over the economics curriculum in the United Kingdom, Australia, the United States and other places[14] has been founded on these narrowing definitional terrains. These limitations amplified in 2007 when the sub-prime mortgage market in the United States collapsed and a Global Financial Crisis was unleashed. This crisis can be traced to cavalier economic decisions that enabled reckless market rules and regulations. Despite this correlation, the confounded gasp of economists who did not predict the crash or have an immediate grasp on its causes was deafening. In some commentary 'another approach has been to simply deny that macroeconomists failed to foresee the crisis'[15] in an attempt to sustain economics as essential to decision-making. The failure of experts to foresee or to take responsibility for this crisis represents a global 'post-content'[16] hierarchy where people in power and institutional authorities simply exist as a placeholder for that power without actually possessing qualifications, the will or the ability to act with authority, integrity or accountability. Baudrillard confirms these 'victories of form and interface management over content and information literacies'.[17] The cultivation of a perverse elitism nestles inside the kernels of a post-content expertise to form an alliance where scholarly thinking and critical consciousness are divorced from authority and from the real conditions within which people live their lives. There is widening scepticism directed towards the infrastructures of information, education, knowledge and expertise that frame the truth-telling mechanisms of our reality and service our lingering enlightenment and neoliberal visions of modernity, social mobility and justice. In the age of information, battles are raging over what it means to be informed. Accusations of ignorance aim to demean the uneducated, underinformed or illiterate while simultaneously scepticism and mistrust is directed towards elite experts.

A common thread reverberating through the post-shock alarm of the election of Donald Trump in the United States, and the Brexit result in the United Kingdom, has been the activation of ignorance via an intricate tethering of racist, sexist and homophobic attitudes to a lack of education as core catalyst for these outcomes. The stupidity of voters is conjured as explanation. This is particularly connected to the perceived victimhood and resentment of poor, white voters. Commentators lament, 'if the Trump era has taught us anything, it's that large numbers of white people in the United States are motivated at least in part by racism in the voting booth'.[18] Our information era disappears in such statements, diverse literacies and critical thinking collapse. The implications of an imagined yet enlightened and informed populace sits at odds with a citizenry that appears to be voting and acting against their own interests. Ignorance is cited as the motivational factor in these problematic acts of public agency.

> *Overall, whites with a four-year college degree or more education made up 30% of all validated voters. Among these voters, far more (55%) said they voted for Clinton than for Trump (38%). Among the much larger group of white voters who had not completed college (44% of all voters), Trump won by more than two-to-one (64%–28%).*[19]

Donald Trump's clear disdain for intellect and the fear-mongering of Brexit campaigners sit at the core of an explanatory network that nestles a culture of ignorance into reactionary and reductive responses of racism, sexism and homophobia. Yet, we have untold levels of access to obscure, specialised and expert information with the arrival of the internet, the ubiquity of broadband technology and diversifying online literacies. More people are completing high school and heading to university. In Australia, the 2016 census reported that 'close to one quarter (24 percent) of youths and adults [had]... completed a bachelor degree or above, up from 18 percent a decade ago'.[20] *The Guardian* reported that by the end of the 1970s in the United Kingdom 14% of school leavers were attending university, increasing dramatically to 40% in 2016.[21] Experts suggest that a high school education 'is not enough'[22] and hint that even a university degree might be inadequate[23] to secure employment in increasingly competitive markets – stimulating more student enrolments at all levels of the educational milieu. The data demonstrates that greater proportions of people are being educated. However, the accusations of ignorance fly when unexpected and socially tremulous conditions erupt. Most surprisingly, this abuse has not been levelled at teachers or educational institutions who most often bear the brunt for failing the expectations of wider society. The crises of education have been on repeat for long enough. Now the lens is focused on white voters – most notably, poor, white voters – whose neat embodiment of impoverishment, resentment and ignorance creates a crucible of concern mashed together with disdain and pity.

The implication is that Trump voters and their kin in the Brexit vote responded as an 'issue of relative deprivation and a feeling of being "left behind" in society'.[24] Their feeling of 'being left behind' it is implied, is due to their inability to leverage educational capital to harness the triumphant glories of globalisation. They are stuck in the past pining for a 'great' America or a resurgent Empire, and their deprivation is a result of clinging to this lost past and not embracing a cosmopolitan, multiculturally literate and diverse identity. The truth is far different. These poor communities are often composed of complex demographics, filled with diversities and differences, as well as unsanctioned literacies. In their Brexit research, Winlow and Hall demonstrated that these communities hold little truck with facile global complexities.

> *We saw precious little of the fruits of privilege on display on the housing estates of Midlands and Northern England. Nor did our respondents seek to return to an age of Empire; for the most part our respondents knew little or nothing about the British Empire. They didn't talk longingly of it because they didn't talk about it at all. Their concerns were about the present and the future.*[25]

Normalised in the accusatory rhetoric is the lower levels of education within these globally alienated working class communities. According to United States PEW data for example, 64% of white non-college graduates voted for Trump.[26] This data is used as a seductive quantitative affirmation of voter educational attributes when paralleled with the 38% of white college graduates who did vote for him. But 77% of non-white non-college graduates voted for Clinton. The rhetoric that normalises dark skin, poverty and a lack of education ignores the complex rationales that motivate voting patterns. The connections between white skin and Trump support is coded as the 'anomaly' that needs to be understood by analysts. Such attitudes are exemplified in articles like 'Understanding White Polarization in the 2016 Vote for President: The Sobering Role of Racism and Sexism'.

> *While Donald Trump enjoyed just a four-point margin over Hillary Clinton among whites with a college degree, his advantage among non-college-educated whites was nearly 40 points. This gap between college-educated and non-college-educated whites was possibly the single most important divide documented in 2016, and it was the culmination of an increasing divide in party identification among college-educated and non-college-educated whites following Obama's election in 2008.*[27]

White people harbouring racist and sexist views in the present could only be caused by a lack of education. That we live in a world where racist, sexist and homophobic views are encouraged, validated and exchanged is at odds with the enlightened, modern, progressive and civilised vision those in affluent contexts have constructed for themselves – a vision that includes the therapeutic potential of education to cure the excesses of attitude that occasionally erupt through the illusion of enlightenment and the callousness of capitalism.

Capitalism cultivates a 'paranoiac economy' – a self-closing system of sense-making that promotes anxiety because 'paranoia already exists as an interpretation'[28] and nothing escapes its pull. This is a 'predatory capitalism' that trades fears and provokes primal preservation. It is 'where the "I" is perceived as good, everything outside the "I" – perceived as external to this "I" – is regarded as the repository of destruction, and it is where the subject expels its own impropriety and vomits up its turmoil'.[29] Education cannot penetrate it. It cannot be rationalised. Instead, experience, opinion and the self becomes the standard for sense-making – an internally resilient system that is shielded from external interventions. The contradictions between the internal desires commodified by capitalism and the external competition that it reifies via racism, sexism, homophobia and ableism perpetuates prejudice, bigotry and even hate into the fabric of the everyday.

> *Such a separation of the inside and outside demands interpretive delusions or a form of wilful ignorance that prevents the development of moral agency. This is because the ego is cut off*

> *from the historical memory of the larger social order as well as from its capacity for imaginative production, since it cannot admit to or acknowledge the illusory nature of the world that it has created.*[30]

Paranoia and wilful ignorance cultivates a rejection of expertise in favour of responsiveness, opinion and experiential rejoinders in contemporary interactions. This manifests a malignment of education to produce anything other than tradable skills for immediate use in a changeable economy. Temporalities of change and histories of heritage are marginalised as outmoded and irrelevant to immediate needs. No internal world or complex subjectivity can be conjured in this information space. This is not a crisis of information, nor what people know at any one time in history. Rather, it is an ambivalence towards expertise and knowing, or as Tom Nichols frames it, an 'indifference to established knowledge'[31] which via crisis morphs into 'a positive *hostility* to such knowledge'.[32] This hostility is propelled by the crumbling currencies of a formal education through which success, prosperity and social mobility are no longer accessible. The rising cascade of unstable employment structures means that the privileges of credentialing ring hollow in the current neoliberal market-place. Expertise has demonstrated itself to be unreliable, askance and wrong. This awkward relationship to knowledge is a crisis of memory in a time when there is an abundance of records, archives and resources but uneven skills with which to access and interpret them.

Official archives service the nation-state, recording important moments, decrees, laws, social movements, policies, significant memoirs, photographs, films and stories. This stacking, listing, cataloguing and administering of official documents, recordings and ephemera in preservation is not only about structuring the past but imagining and investing in the 'future'. This process is also pregnant with fear about the shape that future will take. The anxiety of lost knowledge and its consequences punctuates the archive. The close of the Roman Empire resulted in civilisational collapse marked by 'an extended crisis of governance, civility, economic productivity, technological sophistication and cultural vibrancy, such that post-Roman Europe – the period after about 400 AD – seems to have been a significantly less stable and developed place than it had previously been'.[33] This slide backwards into violence and barbarity is claimed to be caused by the loss of knowledge initiated by a calamity in the movement of populations at the end of Empire.

> *In other words, it seems as though the benefits of long-distance trade and access to foreign 'experts' supplanted local skills and knowledge during the Empire's outward march, but, when access to these networks was cut off, local systems could not maintain*

> *standards, and thus fell back to pre-Roman levels of cultural, social and technological sophistication... a general deterioration following the collapse of imperial power, including the loss of productive capacity at the level of food production, shrinking and more divided, hostile and isolated populations, a loss of scale and complexity in the built environment and, perhaps most tellingly, a retrenchment of literacy and education, all of which seem to have fallen into a steep decline and stayed at a substantially reduced level for a number of centuries.*[34]

Horsley, Kotzé and Hall argue that an increase in violence and brutality is a 'foundation for social relations' during this period.[35] These interactions present an intersecting network of geopolitical relations, population flows, local knowledge and education as essential to sustainable growth. Local literacies and global expertise were fragmented, obscured and obstructed. Horsley, Kotzé and Hall observe 'a remarkable decline in general literacy as common written records ... all but disappeared'[36] during this period and reappeared with the re-emergence of record keeping in the later middle ages connected with the movement towards 'modernity' and the values of progressive 'civilization'. The centralisation of violence within monarchies and regimes (rather than dispersed amongst the population) enabled the stabilisation of commerce and trade facilitated by legal codes and other bureaucratic regulations, which are founded upon the structures of record keeping, archiving and literacy. Modernity deploys these records to map and track 'progress'. The politics of preservation which comes with archiving asserts a hierarchy upon what types of knowledge is considered valuable to the civilising, progressive and future-looking tendencies of the project. There is continuity in memory – what types of things are remembered (and an organised forgetting) – contributes to the foundational narratives of nation-states as they emerge and the projects of imperialism that serve to justify the greatness (as evidenced by their 'progress' and enlightenment) of one nation, region or locality over another.

For modernity to be birthed as 'the age of instrumental reason'[37] rooting out the 'intellectual errors of the past'[38] in excoriation of oppression and domination required a backward-looking lens in order to 'enlighten' the future. History emerges as a discipline drawing on the archive to provide this lens. So, while modernity was considered a 'break' with the past, the requirement of self-consciousness in order to motivate innovation and newness hailed history and situated it in a precarious tension between 'liberalism and rationalism'.[39] The literacies of collective memory as an organised forgetting are internalised within History as a discipline, though not without reflexivity of this process, its strategies and structures. Today, the relevance of History lies in its double-folded facility in both organising the past, but also acknowledging the power structures that provide the tools to make sense of and reify these relationships; like archives. What is remembered, how we remember and why we remember are tethered to a complex dance with modernity. The national archive folds the practices of History into the interests of the nation-state and the lies that need to be told to create coherence – in consciousness, identity, subjectivity, citizenry and society.

The fear of ignorance and the crisis of information are found in disciplinarity debates. The cries against academic 'silos' is a fear of isolation, wilful ignorance and decline. It is a marked shift away from the reverence for silos within early modernity that defined an expertise as a precise, whole and focused knowledge. Such assertions are now considered elitist, marginalising and limiting in late modernity. The persistence of disciplines remains as the old knowledges retain their resonance and the spaces of History and English Literature, for example, are able to conceal their origins and marionette their allegiance to a performative 'enlightenment'. These projects are enfolded in the emergence of modernity and its progressive tendencies that manifested in conquering and pillaging foreign lands under the colonial guise of civilising otherness. History as a discipline of remembering and forgetting has its origins in occidental imaginings.

> *Originating in natural law theory from the sixteenth century onwards, western linear universal history was constituted by and remains largely embedded within the modern civilizational framework, which modern historians and history served to shape. 'History' is a cultural artifact of the modern West.*[40]

This project is expansive to the extent that '[k]nowledge of history, nature, language, literature, geography, society and education were all produced in the context of colonial/imperial relations and the corresponding Occidental imaginary'.[41] These are enlightenment projects cohering as disciplines around and through a human development project. Similarly, English Literature is born out of the necessity to record exchanges, trades, credits and debits in burgeoning industrialism and the germination of capitalism.

> *'English Literature', as a discipline of study that is formulated and consolidated in our universities, for instance, is inaugurated in a specific political economy and one that is associated with British control of India and other geographical terrains.*[42]

The imperialist modernity that slid beneath the surfaces of 'enlightenment' progress and innovation revelled in power, control and conquering while claiming these barbarities in the name of civilisation. It was a demonstration of European civility while delivering it to the so-called uncivilised barbarians of the 'East', the South and other 'dark' places. The currency of national archives is instrumental to these projects as the places where time and space are regulated and contained. The records, items and documents that fill out the administrative backbone of imperialism are catalogued and serve to perpetuate these ways of thinking across the globe in scaffolding imperial power as decolonisation morphs into a postcolonial consciousness.

The postcolonial world emerges in a radical reconfiguration of what it is possible to know and understand, how power is projected and understood as well as what it means to be 'civilised'. It is impossible for Empire to shape and shine itself as a productive and progressive project. Instead, its traumas, perversities and barbarities are aired. The incivility of oppression, the casual murder, rape and terror have nothing to do with enlightenment but are enacted in its name. The postcolonial cannot allow these narratives to exist unchallenged. They strip them bare and revel in competing memories and experiences that deny the pretension of enlightened civilising modernity. Decolonisation is about folding back those narratives to reveal the terrifying underbelly of imperial ideologies that leverage enlightenment and archival articulations to make invasion palatable, exploitation natural and terror beneficial. The educated scaffolds upon which these knowledges and attitudes were built are retained in the absence of a radical decolonising project. It is at this point archives can be put to different use and radical thinking can emerge. The dynamic dance between pasts and presents mediated by the archive and through records that contain, limit and shape what is known and how it is known cohere the complexities by which information enters into public consciousness. Access is complex, requiring literacies that are compounded, stringent and detailed. In current neoliberal economic outlooks, these literacies have been colonised by work-ready attributes or functional skills. Social consciousness has been hijacked by neoliberal economisation, and educational institutions have abandoned their role in assessing, designing, interpreting and engaging in difficult thinking in substitute for short-term pay-offs in labour exchange. Industrial, postcolonial, imperial, regional and global interfaces play out in the everyday real where intuitive intelligence circulates but interpretive reasoning is muted by a mistrust of expertise. These experiences are in tension with the dominating disciplines that fold into elite interests in service of disenfranchising the local expertise and organic intelligence of communities and interests interfacing with the everyday real.

NOTES

1. Gavan Butler, *Evan Jones, and Frank Stilwell, Political Economy Now!: The Struggle for Alternative Economics at the University of Sydney* (Sydney: Darlington Press, 2009), 6.
2. The University of Manchester Post-Crash Economics Society, *Economics, Education and Unlearning: Economics Education at the University of Manchester*, (Foreword by Andrew Haldane), (Manchester: Post-Crash Economics Society at the University of Manchester, 2014), 7, http://www.post-crash economics.com/economics-education-and-unlearning/.
3. The University of Manchester Post-Crash Economics Society, *Economics, Education and Unlearning*, 7.
4. These two crises in economics education shared a common foundation. Bruce Williams, the Vice Chancellor at the University of Sydney who presided over the appointments of Hogan and Simkin had been a professor of economics at the University of Manchester from 1959–1966.
5. Luca Mavelli, "Citizenship for Sale and the Neoliberal Political Economy of Belonging," *International Studies Quarterly* 62, (2018): 482.
6. Joe Earle, Cahal Moran, and Zach Ward-Perkins, *The Econocracy: On the Perils of Leaving Economics to the Experts* (London: Penguin Random House, 2017), 3.
7. Binyamin Applebaum, *The Economists' Hour: How the False Prophets of Free Markets Fractured our Society*, (London: Picador, 2019).
8. Earle, Moran, and Ward-Perkins, *The Econocracy*, 12.
9. Earle, Moran, and Ward-Perkins, *The Econocracy*, 16.
10. Earle, Moran, and Ward-Perkins, *The Econocracy*, 18.
11. Aeron Davis, *Reckless Opportunists: Elites at the End of the Establishment* (Manchester: Manchester University Press, 2018), 89.
12. Earle, Moran, and Ward-Perkins, *The Econocracy*, 48.
13. Rik Pieters and Hans Baumgartner, "Who talks to whom?: Intra- and Interdisciplinary Communication of Economics Journals," *Journal of Economic Literature* 40, no. 2, (2002): 504.
14. There are now multiple post-crash economics societies including Post-Crash Economics at the London School of Economics, Glasgow University Real World Economics Society, Cambridge Society for Economic Pluralism, Institute for New Economic Thinking, Edinburgh University Society for Economic Pluralism, Real World Economics at Bristol, New School Economics at Goldsmiths, Aberdeen Political Economy Group, Greenwich Pluralism in Economics, Kingston University Rethinking Economics, Open Economics Leeds, Newcastle Economics Society, Rethinking Economics Oxford, Alternative Economics Society Sheffield, Open Economics Forum SOAS (School of Oriental and African Studies University of London), Pluralist Economics at Sussex, and Better Economics University College London.
15. Earle, Moran, and Ward-Perkins, *The Econocracy*, 70.
16. Tara Brabazon, Steve Redhead, and Runyararo S. Chivaura, *Trump Studies: An Intellectual Guide to Why Citizens Vote Against Their Interests* (Bingley: Emerald: 2019), 17.
17. Brabazon, Redhead, and Chivaura, *Trump Studies*, 17.

18. Noah Berlatsky, "Trump Voters Motivated by Racism may be Violating the Constitution: Can they be stopped?" *NBC News: Think*, January 17, 2020. https://www.nbcnews.com/think/opinion/trump-voters-motivated-racism-may-be-violating-constitution-can-they-ncna1110356.
19. PEW Research Center, "For Most Trump Voters, 'Very Warm' Feelings for Him Endure: An Examination of the 2016 Electorate, Based on Validated Voters," *PEW Research Center U.S. Politics and Policy*, August 9, 2018, https://www.people-press.org/2018/08/09/an-examination-of-the-2016-electorate-based-on-validated-voters/.
20. Australian Bureau of Statistics, "Australian's Pursuing Higher Education in Record Numbers," October 23, 2017, https://www.abs.gov.au/AUSSTATS/abs@.nsf/mediareleasesbyReleaseDate/1533FE5A8541D66CCA2581BF00362D1D.
21. Liz Lightfoot, "The Student Experience: Then and Now," *The Guardian*, June 24, 2016, https://www.theguardian.com/education/2016/jun/24/has-university-life-changed-student-experience-past-present-parents-vox-pops.
22. R. Wayne Branch, *High School is Not Enough: What Are You Going To Do About It?* (North Charleston: Rama Publications, 2013).
23. Evan Ortlieb, "Just Graduating from University is No Longer Enough to Get a Job," *The Conversation*, February 12, 2015, https://theconversation.com/just-graduating-from-university-is-no-longer-enough-to-get-a-job-36906.
24. Paul B. Hutchings and Katie E. Sullivan, "Prejudice and the Brexit Vote: A Tangled Web," *Palgrave Communications* 5, no. 5, (2019): 3, https://doi.org/10.1057/s41599-018-0214-5.
25. Steve Hall and Simon Winlow, "Why the Left Must Change: Right-Wing Populism in Context," in *Progressive Justice in an Age of Repression: Strategies for Challenging the Rise of the Right*, eds. Walter S. DeKeseredy and Elliott Currie (London: Routledge, 2019), 26–41.
26. PEW Research Center, "For Most Trump voters."
27. Brian F. Schaffner, Matthew Mcwilliams, and Tatishe Nteta, "Understanding White Polarization in the 2016 Vote for President: The Sobering Role of Racism and Sexism," *Political Science Quarterly* 133, no. 1, (Spring 2018): 9–34, https://doi.org/10.1002/polq.12737.
28. Peter McLaren, *Che Guevara, Paulo Freire, and the Pedagogy of Revolution* (Lanham: Rowman and Littlefield, 2000), 30.
29. McLaren, *Che Guevara, Paulo Freire, and the Pedagogy of Revolution*, 30.
30. McLaren, *Che Guevara, Paulo Freire, and the Pedagogy of Revolution*, 31.
31. Tom Nichols, *The Death of Expertise: The Campaign Against Established Knowledge and Why it Matters* (Oxford: Oxford University Press, 2019), 20.
32. Nichols, *The Death of Expertise*, 20.
33. Mark Horsley, Justin Kotzé, and Steve Hall, "The Maintenance of Orderly Disorder: Modernity, Markets and the Pseudo-Pacification Process," *Journal of European History of Law* 6, no. 1, (2015): 4 http://insight.cumbria.ac.uk/id/eprint/1949/1/Horsley_TheMaintenanceOfOrderly.pdf.
34. Horsley, Kotzé, and Hall, "The Maintenance of Orderly Disorder: Modernity, Markets and the Pseudo-Pacification Process," 5.
35. Horsley, Kotzé, and Hall, "The Maintenance of Orderly Disorder," 6.
36. Horsley, Kotzé, and Hall, "The Maintenance of Orderly Disorder," 5.

37. Philip K. Lawrence, "Enlightenment, modernity and war," *History of the Human Sciences* 12, no. 1, (1999): 6.
38. Lawrence, "Enlightenment, modernity and war," 5.
39. Michael A. Peters, "The University and the New Humanities: Professing with Derrida," *Arts and Humanities in Higher Education* 3, no. 1, (2004): 46, https://doi.org/10.1177/14740222040396446.
40. Michael Baker, "Modernity/Coloniality and Eurocentric Education: Towards a Post-Occidental Self-Understanding of the Present," *Policy Futures in Education* 10, no. 1, (2012): 7. http://dx.doi.org/10.2304/pfie.2012.10.1.4.
41. Baker, "Modernity/Coloniality and Eurocentric Education," 12.
42. Thomas Docherty, *Literature and Capital* (New York: Bloomsbury, 2018), 29.

2

THE LADS: A REBELLIOUS REFUSAL OF RESILIENCE

In the sense, therefore, that I argue that it is their own culture which most effectively prepares some working-class lads for the manual giving of their labour power we may say that there is an element of self-damnation in the taking on of subordinate roles in Western capitalism. However, this damnation is experienced, paradoxically, as true learning, affirmation, appropriation, and as a form of resistance... there is an objective basis for these subjective feelings and cultural processes. They involve a partial penetration of the really determining conditions of existence of the working class which are definitely superior to those official versions of their reality which are proffered through the school and various state agencies. It is only on the basis of such real cultural articulation with their conditions that groups of working-class lads come to take a hand in their own damnation. The tragedy and contradiction is that these forms of 'penetration' are limited, distorted and turned back on themselves, often unintentionally, by complex processes ranging from both general ideological processes and those within the school and guidance agencies to the widespread influence of a form of patriarchal male domination and sexism within working-class culture itself.[1]

In the 1970s, Paul Willis asked why working-class lads choose working-class labour. *Learning to Labour* was ground-breaking research into how working-class resistance to middle-class education was actually undermining students' capacity for social mobility and movement into more affluent and empowered contexts. The irreverent resistances of the working-class lads presented a 'tragedy' that constrained rather than liberated them from the conditions of their everyday life enfolded in instability and narrowing opportunities. The lads traded social mobility for personal mobility within the school – truancy and self-direction – in rebellion against the formal authority structures embraced by the staff who sought to impose an ethos of education accessible via correct behaviours, manners and obscure codifications of appropriate 'respect'. In education, '[t]here is relatively little direct coercion or oppression but an enormous constriction of the range of moral possibilities'[2] for the lads. This tightly controlled 'moral basis for the educational exchange'[3] is founded on ideals that simultaneously confirm the limitations of opportunities for an unruly working class, while offering them a pathway into affluence and certitude built upon rejection of working-class cultural traits. These lads were expected to enter into the middle class by unquestioningly embracing the traits of enlightened modernity via civilising tropes of good manners and appropriate behaviour – structures that are constantly mobile and limiting – while also denuding themselves of their known literacies to embrace foreign ones.

The sabotage of social mobility by the lads created a conundrum. As a pathway to opportunity, educational methods needed to be revisited and revised to enable access for these working-class communities. However, social mobility hides its tenuousness by being disguised as an inherently benevolent trajectory of enlightened opportunity. Social mobility is most often configured as individual success enacted through the conduit of education enabling a transition from a low social-economic situation into a higher one (though it also operates in reverse). As soon as consciousness of class is endowed through education, it is expected that the working class would want to shed their oppressions as an inevitable part of being awoken into middle-class opportunities. It is in these definitions that the narrowing of enlightened ideals is unmasked, for as E.P. Thompson has noted, the working classes were far from uneducated or lacking in motivation and drive.

> *For the first half of the nineteenth century, when the formal education of a great part of the people entailed little more than instruction in the Three R's was by no means a period of intellectual atrophy. The towns, and even the villages, hummed with the energy of the autodidact. Given the elementary techniques of literacy, labourers, artisans, shopkeepers and clerks and schoolmasters proceeded to instruct themselves, severally or in groups.*[4]

Thompson reminds readers that 'illiteracy (we should remember) by no means excluded men from political discourse'.[5] Yet, today the end-game of entry into the middle class is rarely questioned as a liberation, the acquisition of critical thinking and a transformation of opportunity. This aspiration reaffirms the emphasis on individual choice, flexible subjectivity and independent affluence dressed up as collective change and universal mobility towards betterment. Attaining middle-class status via an education for exchange makes life easier and less burdensome. Moving people out of labour-intensive and corporeally tenuous work and into safer, more cerebral and sustainable employment that offers respite and access to increasing affluence is an important but closed endeavour. It can affirm and sustain the structures of oppression that promote differential access to power. It is hard to argue against such achievements without appearing to condemn working-class people to a life of hard labour and financial insecurity. Yet the changes to middle-class work means that it too is now defined by instability and precarity.[6] These instabilities are compounded now that neoliberal atomisation has counteracted the buttressing effect of communal structures that insulated against the cold realities of social change. In the twentieth century as the middle class has expanded[7] and offered increasing financial stability and improved quality of life for many people, working-class communities have been corroded by ongoing attacks against their livelihoods. These corrosions were against the solidarities and support structures.

Fundamental social and political shifts involving a push towards 'raising the aspirations of young people [and others] from disadvantaged backgrounds, rather than direct measures to reduce inequality'[8] affirms social mobility as an individual attribute of success and independence. The lads' embrace of working-class models of success (entailing a required and expected rebellion and resistance to the middle class), presents a site for a radical reification of exploitation (within and via working-class ethics), but also functions as a refusal of social mobility and the ideals that present entry into the middle class as desirable.

> However, although educational attainment remains an important determinant of achieved status, evidence suggests that its contribution to social mobility in the United Kingdom has not increased as liberal theory predicts. There are two key reasons for this: firstly, class-based inequalities in education have persisted rather stubbornly; and secondly, the influence of educational attainment on achieved status has remained stable, or even diminished, between cohorts born since the mid-twentieth

century. Similar trends are evident in other OECD nations, calling into question the assumption that western societies will increasingly be transformed into education-based meritocracies.[9]

It is in the interests of capitalism to retain and perpetuate class-based differences. Education functions as a buffer to this cold reality, presenting a strategy of displacement and delay to the inequalities that await graduates in an unfair employment environment, where job scarcity functions to drive up demand and reduce wages. Education as a conduit to better livelihoods is destabilised in these relationships. Entry into the middle class means an intimate and unquestioning compliance to accelerated capitalism and its forms of domination and exploitation, which have been masked precisely because the language of class-based exploitation has left our lexicon.

Schools undermine working-class students' potentials and possibilities with the deployment of striated ethics and moral certitudes about correct behaviours, manners and 'respect'. The students differentiate themselves by rebelling, and once this transformation is initiated 'there is a powerful cultural charge behind him [the lad] to complete this process'[10] in normalised community and home-life attitudes and investments. The inadequate and inflexible tropes of educational repertoires codify normalities of oppression and restriction, straight-jacketing students into a moral pathway of enlightened modernity at all costs – to become a particularly type of subject that is removed from the cache of consciousness currently codified in their everyday. The rebellions of the lads aimed at crafting their own time and space outside of the structures of schooling temporalities and realities. For Willis, modern education is unable to overcome or transform the indoctrinating and performative effects of working-class culture by codifying sedate modern ideals that victimise and punish these identities. Official narratives and institutions assert truths and realities that have very little to do with the actual conditions of working-class experience. Instead, deploying those that ultimately reconfirm archetypal working-class roles and responsibilities thereby stabilises structures of oppression. Willis was calling for an interrogation of 'the real' for these working-class lads and to identify how the superimposed constructs were alienating on a variety of axes. Willis speculated that access to this 'real' could open up trajectories for radical pedagogies that could move educational tropes away from their proclivity to reproduce class differences.

A struggle over education is being waged – one upon which the order of society is being contested and defended. The lads performed their own double refusals by simultaneously deploying cleverness in their rebellion but refusing that intelligence within formalised education.

> Though 'the lads' usually resist conventional ways of showing their abilities, certainly the ablest likes to be thought of as 'quick'. Certain cultural values, like fast talking and humour, do anyway register in some academic subjects. Joey, for instance, walks a very careful tightrope in English between 'laffing' with 'the lads' and doing the occasional 'brilliant' essay. In certain respects, obvious stupidity is penalised more heavily amongst 'the lads' than by staff, who 'expected nothing better'.[11]

Education confirms the ideological positioning of the working-class lads and reinforces their trajectories into laborious trades. These meanings are embraced by the working-class lads and affirmed by their teachers who fail to see the complexities in the rebellions or to see them as living, evolving ways of interfacing with power. By framing education was the pathway out of difficult conditions and towards a better standard of living for these students, and not identifying how this movement required the embrace of equally destructive and potentially problematic subjectivities, the double refusal cannot be realised. By enacting 'resistance', these students were seen to be sabotaging their lives rather than deploying a complex potentiality – a refusal to be dominated and a refusal to dominate.

These students recognised the middle-class tropes of education offering a pathway of progress and civility only if they subjected themselves to new forms of domination and rejected the networks and knowledges they already had easy access to. This does not absolve the working-class lads or community as an authentic intervention into the exchanges of domination. Willis mapped the racist, sexist and violent literacies, initiated and traded within working-class culture. These were performed to buffer the seductions of middle-class affluence as a pretence of liberation only to be exchanged for different forms of domination. The lads were interjecting their own refusals. They were refusing to be dominated by teachers and the school system as well as refusing the domination on offer where an exchange of self-for-power was enacted. They rejected the 'earoles' – middle-class, effete or privileged students as part of an affirmation of working-class identity. They also marginalised Asian and black students among their cohort. Willis demonstrated the everyday brutalities that serviced a display of autonomy and terror. 'There is a positive joy in fighting, in causing fights through intimidation, in talking about fighting and about the tactics of the whole fight situation'.[12] The lads were also not rejecting or refusing capitalism. Willis identified 'certain stylistic/symbolic discourses'[13] embraced by them in their rebellion against authority, namely 'clothes, cigarettes and alcohol.'[14] The lads were not rejecting power or domination, but they were refusing to be dominated and to embrace the domination that sought to disempower them. Social mobility as a desirable pathway into these forms of domination was expressly rejected.

Willis' work was a boon for educational theorists who used his insights to understand school cultures and the importance of connecting to the contexts in which students were experiencing learning, including the economy and the community. Reifying the importance of working-class culture to effective pedagogy opened up pathways for thinking about students from diverse backgrounds, abilities and embodiments and their complex interfaces with educational hierarchies. In 2004, *Learning to Labour in New Times* revisited Willis' work in a radically changed economy of accelerated capitalism and neoliberal politics. Stanley Aronowitz's foreword crystallised the ambivalence towards social mobility, not as an active sabotage of opportunity, but as a critical recognition and rejection of the seductions of the middle class when he wrote of the (new) working class: 'they have learned that the academic promises for social mobility have proven to be ephemeral'.[15] The seductions sold to cultivate good workers for a capitalist economy are built on striation and suppression. During industrialism, ideals of honour in labour served this function. Ambivalence characterises the conditions of an accelerated capitalist rise of technical, financial and service employment that has dislodged the traditional terrains of work. Focussing on students and their aspirations over state-based interventions into inequality was about 'emphasising equality of opportunity as opposed to equality of outcome'.[16] Today, these ideals are found in self-directed instruction, flipped classrooms and student-centred learning that focus on the technicalities of tuition by de-emphasising the role of the teacher as arbiter of expertise and reifying the agency of the student. Aspiration and affluence are codified by capitalism to define the cost of entry into the middle class moving from being exploited to becoming the exploiter whilst maintaining the illusion that 'true' power lies elsewhere. This is enfolded into the neoliberal languages of resilience that define the subject as that which makes rational choices for the self to sustain and adapt to instabilities in a destabilising system – displacing and masking structures of power as unpredictable, disastrous and exploitative.

Instead of indoctrination into valued modes of knowing and behaving, what Willis was calling for was a way through the messy metaphors of contemporary education to drill down into the tools and attitudes that can help all students examine their everyday lives to activate intervention in their own circumstances rather than an idealised enlightened subject who can deploy the correct codes to unblock (shrinking) employment opportunities. This project is activated in the contemporary via the trope of critical thinking which is hailed as a cure-all for empowerment. The tenacity with which modes of critical thought have been attached to an interventionist subjectivity and co-opted into economic-based educational repertoires in curricula outcomes means this phrase has been emptied of its potency. Critical thinking is now randomly and routinely deployed as a catch-phrase to assert abstract pedagogic protocols. Few understand what critical thinking is except in its negative – to be censorious or reproving. Alternatively, 'we think of critics as people who have to constantly complain about something as a form of scepticism that can sometimes lead to cynicism'.[17] Cynical scepticism often substitutes for critical thinking when people are confronted with challenges to their perception of a common sense 'real'. Critical literacy is currently overestimated. Instead, judgement rather than discernment dominates ways of knowing. This judgement is connected to internal experience rather than abstract thought. Empathising with specific identity experiences of victimhood has stood in for unpacking the political and economic processes and ideas that structure uneven access to power and the perpetuation of exploitation because education has abandoned these complexities in favour of replicating neoliberal structures of sense-making and seductions of the self. The experience of marginalisation has buffeted against a system that assures equal opportunity and meritocratic success is to be found in hard work, application and persistence. In capitalism, exploitation is traded and exchanged, and success is built upon the marginalisation of specific groups so others can prosper.

The rise in cynicism is tethered to a widening distrust of experts and a configuring of expertise as niche knowledge unconnected to 'the real'. It is part of a repertoire of expression that masks the conditions of economic exploitation that blight people's everyday lives. Included in this lexicon is the rising popularity of sustainability and resilience, most notably ideas located in the educational ideologies of student-centred learning. Dislocating knowledge from an inevitable march towards elitism and transforming it into personalised platform for everyday repertoires of rebellion, resistance and recognition, resilience has become the functional outcome of educational efficacy and interests. An abstract movement from an ineffective modern subject situated within social change, intervention, improvement and progress towards neoliberal subjects whose internal and personal betterment and aspirational repertoire is elevated as the desired progress in a laissez faire approach to social growth, marks a complex interfacing of modern neoliberalism funnelled through contemporary knowledge making and the function of education. The rise of the resilient subject and the alignment of educational outcomes towards sustainability – which while a potent discourse of disruption in a capitalism built upon resource extraction and exploitation of the land as well as climate change denial – in education, it services neoliberal models of selfhood and society. These ideals of sustainability are not just those located in an ecological exchange of balanced inputs and outputs in service of intervening in environmental crises. They expand to account for human character and shape the individual as a sustainable person, who acts to manage themselves in a society largely out of their own control and understanding.

The (neo)liberal subject is defined as the model of contemporary personhood – fully formed, critically enabled and internally rich – equipped with the tools of intellect to make wise and sustainable choices. Late modernity values frameworks of flexibility, adaptability and the fluid flows of accelerated capitalism where the outcomes of progress, change and improvement remain, though with emphasis onto the self rather than the state. The 'modern liberal subject was assumed to have the will and capacity to act on and to transform, to secure and to know its external world'.[18] Today, the 'neoliberal subject can only understand the subject as increasingly differentiated in its choice-making vulnerability, rather than as a potential collectivity'.[19] An emphasis on control over the internal world and the efficacy of choices and changes defines this neoliberal 'enlightened' subject. The power over personal choice is framed as only having consequences at the limits of the body and so displaces or 'deliberalises' debate by divesting 'security responsibilities from the level of the state down to the level of the citizen'.[20] The intimate tethering of civilising progress, innovation and change with social betterment is entwined with individual improvement tropes and the role of education in lifting the subject out of their lot and offering transformation of the self and society as a consequence of these individual choices. To create a resilient society that is adaptable, flexible and complex is often cited as a desired outcome for a diverse and progressive education structure. Such rhetoric accounts for the differing needs of diverse groups and the complexities within which life is lived and realised. However, this style of expressing social needs and engagement is coated in the tropes of neoliberal capitalism whereby resilience is deployed to craft a liberal subjectivity that normalises and centralises disaster, trauma and difficulty as the dominant mode of contemporary existence. Resilience is defined as an essential literacy that can be used to acknowledge, embrace and move with the difficult and the disastrous autonomously without expecting or demanding intervention from the state or institutions that have relinquished their responsibility for managing or arbitrating disasters which are now a normal part of modern living.

> *The resilient subject is a subject that must permanently struggle to accommodate itself to the world, not a subject that can conceive of*

> *changing the world, its structure and conditions of possibility, but a subject that accepts the disastrousness of the world it lives in as a condition of partaking of that world, which will not question the reasons why he or she suffers but which accepts the necessity of the injunction to change itself in correspondence with the suffering nor presupposed as endemic.*[21]

Adaptability is the desired outcome to create resonant and robust communities of well-being. Education has been co-opted as part of the normalisation and seduction of resilience as a contemporary advantage in modern life. Life-long learning is an example of insurance against the trauma of unemployment. The ever-changing workplace and cascading employment opportunities cannot be mediated by the state but must be embraced by the subject and managed on their own terms, by upskilling their learning, developing new literacies and expanding their credentials. Resilient individuals are defined as intimately connected to their everyday experiences and possess the tools to manage, navigate and endure, whereas experts are disconnected and remote, unconnected to 'the real'. Contemporary education is the thoroughfare for this resilient subject who upskills, trains and learns ever-altering literacies to buffer against the roiling employment marketplace where capitalism is in crisis, and shrinking opportunities create competition and cataclysm. They become resilient without leveraging resilient thinking to make connections between their everyday 'real' and the potential to refuse.

The lads in Willis' study were rejecting the manufactured insertion of resilience that demanded they improve their lives. Instead they were passing an initiation into the communities that offered already sustainable and robust networks (managed by careful consciousness of the correct performance of gendered, raced and sexualised hierarchies). Theirs was a double refusal; a refusal to be dominated by education systems that urged them to reject their origins and a refusal to enter into the trajectories of middle-class domination.

Education is recruited within resilience discourses as a cache of tools that can prepare individuals to manage the upheavals and traumas of the everyday. The working-class lads already had these networks waiting for them after they passed through the schooling system. The individual was included in community structures that would service as part of a resilience repertoire enfolded into identity and infrastructures. In late capitalism, 'the focus of resilience practices is less upon the specific threat or "event" (which can be prepared for or reacted to) and more on the effects of a crisis or disaster at the level of the individual and community'.[22] Education is enfolded in narratives of resilience that prepare students for disastrous and risky events in a time of tremulous outcomes and uneven employment opportunities. Adaptability, flexibility and fluidity are highlighted as desirable graduate outcomes. Resilience is compliance. Education for life-long learning, upskilling, recredentialing is concerned with sustaining the self in an era when the communal structures that would normally interface with the individual have been corroded by capitalism. The crises in employment and the collaboration of educational institutions in providing learning for labour focuses education upon the self to develop buttress against the interruptions and eruptions of accelerated capitalism. Personal resilience, aspiration and social mobility are deployed in educational rhetoric to mask the inequities with which knowledge is being coddled and cauterised to delay and deny radical ways of thinking that refuse.

Recoding education is needed. How and what we choose to teach remains intimately tethered to our imaginings of the future and our ideals of human progress. The intimate relationship between the human subject, enlightenment, progress and modernity has created a network of knowledges that nudge towards outward and inward 'development' defined as resilience now that social mobility has become tenuous. The rising cascade of unstable employment structures means that the privileges of credentialing are ambiguous in the current neoliberal marketplace. Expertise has demonstrated itself in many circumstances to be unreliable in a post-truth world of fake news and where trust of 'post-content' power structures corrodes consciousness. In its place, the code-word of resilience is deployed to shift focus onto the present and the self – to locate the burden of social change within individual choice as if consumer ideologies offer a quick and easy problem-solving framework for all social complexities. What is needed are the tools for double refusal. This is not an education for improvement, of the self or society – these ideals often service power. An education for refusal permits a development of the skills, literacies and critical understandings needed to interrogate the everyday 'real' that produces radically reflective potentials. Critical thinking must morph into radical thinking.

Radical thinking configures temporalities of knowing that determine how 'the real' is conjured and accepted. Radical thinking permits an interrogation of the foundations by which we make sense of this 'real' and the tenets of knowledge that frame truthfulness and expertise. It permits the obscure and unexpected connections needed to problematise resistance and present space for a double refusal. This is more than thinking 'without the help of another'[23] but akin to declaring 'open war on the contemporary bourgeois vision of Western civilized progress'[24] in order to conjure the words and languages of ways of knowing that diversify expertise as a transformation of consciousness. To educate from a place of justice is imperative for a radical thinker. To enact the 'dreams of a revolutionary'[25] and to understand the networks of knowledge that transcend the arbitrary and linear to make room for the ambiguous and the unclear. Understanding how events and happenings become resonant or fade from collective memory is an important part of this process. The hyperlinked and hashtagged online discourse permits the cultivation of radical archives conjured in a negotiation with the moment, the event or the happening in order to process, understand and codify 'the real'. A struggle over the dominant narratives, meanings and memories is occurring in these interactions where the crowd-sourced syllabus is conjured to organise, manage and distribute styles of knowing in perverse alliances and connections that open up the possibilities for the double refusal.

NOTES

1. Paul Willis, *Learning to Labour: How Working Class Kids Get Working Class Jobs* (Aldershot: Ashgate, 1997/1978), 3.
2. Willis, *Learning to Labour*, 66.
3. Willis, *Learning to Labour*, 80.
4. E. P. Thompson, *The Making of the English Working Class* (London: Penguin, 1980/1963), 781–782.
5. Thompson, *The Making of the English Working Class*, 782.
6. Guy Standing, *The Precariat: The New Dangerous Class* (London: Bloomsbury, 2011).
7. The Brookings Institute claimed in 2018 that "just over 50 percent of the world's population, or some 3.8 billion people, live in households with enough discretionary expenditure to be considered "middle class or "rich"." Homi Kharas and Kristofer Hamel, "A global tipping point: Half the World is Now Middle Class or Wealthier," *Brookings Institute*, September 27, 2018, https://www.brookings.edu/blog/future-development/2018/09/27/a-global-tipping-point-half-the-world-is-now-middle-class-or-wealthier/. However, this assessment must be tempered with a 2019 OECD report of increasing income disparity and claim that "the middle class dream is increasingly only a dream for many." OECD, *Under Pressure: The Squeezed Middle Class*, (OECD Publishing, 2019), 16, https://doi.org/10.1787/689afed1-en.
8. Ron Thompson and Robin Simmons, "Social Mobility and Post-Compulsory Education: Revisiting Boudon's Model of Social Opportunity," *British Journal of Sociology of Education* 34, nos. 5–6, (2013): 745, http://dx.doi.org/10.1080/01425692.2013.816038.
9. Thompson and Simmons, "Social Mobility and Post-Compulsory Education," 745.
10. Willis, *Learning to Labour*, 74.
11. Willis, *Learning to Labour*, 32.
12. Willis, *Learning to Labour*, 34.
13. Willis, *Learning to Labour*, 17.
14. Willis, *Learning to Labour*, 17.

15. Stanley Aronowitz, "Foreword," in *Learning to Labor in New Times*, eds. Nadine Dolby and Greg Dimitriadis with Paul Willis (New York: Routledge Falmer, 2004), 11–12.
16. Thompson and Simmons, "Social Mobility and Post-Compulsory Education," 744.
17. Peter M. Nardi, *Critical thinking: Tools for Evaluating Research* (Oakland: University of California Press, 2017), 4.
18. David Chandler, "Resilience: Societalization of Security," in David Chandler and Julian Reid, *The Neoliberal Subject: Resilience, Adaptation and Vulnerability* (London: Rowman and Littlefield, 2016), 45.
19. Chandler, "Resilience: Societalization of Security," 43.
20. Chandler, "Resilience: Societalization of Security," 27.
21. Julian Reid, "Resilience: The biopolitics of security," in David Chandler and Julian Reid, *The Neoliberal Subject: Resilience, Adaptation and Vulnerability* (London: Rowman and Littlefield, 2016), 68.
22. Chandler, "Resilience: Societalization of Security," 30.
23. Kenneth Wain, *On Rousseau: An Introduction to his Radical Thinking on Education and Politics* (Rotterdam: Sense Publishers, 2011), 17.
24. Wain, *On Rousseau*, 43.
25. Wain, *On Rousseau*, 42.

3

DISINTERMEDIATING THE ARCHIVES: EVENTAL EDUCATION

Online spaces open vibrant new worlds for exploration. Google has created a banal interface that disguises these possibilities. Behind this banality is a massive regulatory structure dominated by the PageRank algorithm designed to discern the intent of inquiry and return relevant results. According to Siva Vaidhyanathan, 'Google was clean. It was pure. It was simple. It accepted no money for ranking one page higher in a search than another'.[1] This lean paradigm for information organisation and retrieval is attractive in its simplicity. By augmenting the flattened information landscape of the digitised sphere, Google created a revolution in searching by managing 'dynamic hierarchies according to the visibility and importance of each website',[2] allowing users to outsource discernment. Amongst the information glut, Google sorted and categorised information 'by rendering the collective knowledge into a proprietary scale of values'.[3] It provided a means of control in a massive data landscape of information.

The ease with which results are generated absent of effort in an information laborious environment provides seductive simplicity in a world of complexity. These seductions are also systemized in the democratic potentials offered by the Google interface to dislodge the power of elites in managing and controlling what is known. The tensions between the indexing properties of Google and its flattening of the information landscape spotlights the role of literacy in ordering knowledge. Google takes the stresses out of managing, deciding, ranking and retrieving. Yet, it hides the literacies needed to make discernible decisions about the information it returns. The scale of information available is reduced to a manageable return of results, directing attention and cultivating algorithmic attitudes. In this deceptively simple process, it marginalises the complexities within which knowledge is actually created, how it is understood and even stored. Google rents out intellect, fragments it and decontexualises knowing.

This automated and obscured PageRank formula masks the networks of knowledge needed prior to search engine input and to assess the outcomes once the query is clicked.[4] In information overload we have confused quantity with quality and created conditions that obscure the way knowledge enters into circulation and is critiqued.

> *It is important to be completely honest about the internet – let alone the web – that is being searched by Google. The web is large, occasionally irrelevant, filled with advertising, outdated ghost sites and is increasingly corporatized. It seems appropriate that Google is ubiquitous when teachers and librarians are overworked and less available to see students.*[5]

The PageRank algorithm leverages and indexes the asymmetrical, networked rhizomatic relationships between metadata, information and the user at the keyboard. Flitting attention funnelled through accumulated online literacies and socially mediated moments reinforce and ratify the multitude of fragments, sections and slices that we must link, curate and cultivate to craft a bespoke experience of understanding because we can no longer rely on the linearities and coherence of 'education-for-training' to provide the tools for critical thinking. Instead, disintermediation crafts a consciousness of spaces that need to be filled, fragments of knowing and half-truths that require clarification with skills people lack in an education system geared towards skills-based training for work-ready graduation. The skills required to assess, understand, process and provoke are masked behind the priorities of capitalism that requires workers not thinkers.

Disintermediation refers to the way 'links are removed from the traditional supply and distribution chain'[6] in the online environment. This means that traditional gatekeeper functions are being bypassed by a cadre of online media managers, bloggers, convenors and curators who have variable skills of verification and knowledge management to measure and monitor how and when information may enter into common repertoires of knowing. Hierarchies of knowledge are bypassed and even collapse. Traditional mechanisms by which truth and integrity are advanced become skewed. In effect 'a culture of equivalence'[7] emerges where the ability to discern different sources, methodologies and epistemologies and their situation within a hierarchy of knowing is obscured. The networks of disintermediation create complexities where information flows, intersects, collides and diverts in unpredictable ways, creating perverse alliances and connections that permit new connections to be made.

In the hyperlinked online environment blocks of text known as lexia are connected together to create fluidities which 'can always be reconfigured, reformatted, rewritten'.[8] This motivates abstract and undefined beginnings and endings and changes our perceptions of how ideas fit together, are built and are communicated.[9] These relationships are alive and always 'open-ended, expandable and incomplete'[10] delivering many points for new ideas and nodes to be connected, creating new opportunities and outcomes. 'Electronic linking radically changes the experience of a text by changing its spatial and temporal relation to other texts'.[11] These relationships reformulate how information is shaped and shared and alter the meaning, outcomes and purposes of knowledge. Positive and negative outcomes are enfolded in new spaces for different ways of knowing to emerge, including the knowledges embraced and realised by disempowered groups, but also fragmenting continuities which track the evolutions of ideas. Heritage and provenance are disconnected. Information can be hijacked for purpose via a stripping of the context in which that information was generated and defined. Importantly, hyperlinking bypasses the controls and regulations that organises and defines how information is ranked, classified and catalogued such as those enacted by national archives and libraries where the curator would disassemble information into smaller fragments removed from their original contexts so they could be reconstituted under clear and strategic structures of classificatory authority. The 'disciplinary classifications and taxonomies derived from the division of the arts and sciences that ... became refined in the 18th century European Enlightenment'[12] still service the organisation of knowledge today. The archive forms a 'guiding logic'[13] to understanding the historical world; the frames in which information is created and transmitted. It is not just a 'collection of records',[14] but a system of organising, mobilised through the rigour of the curator in their deployment of 'provenance, custody and central authority'[15] that offers up a source of historical truth in the cultivation of the subject at the centre of a national imagining that the archive seeks to service. It is the provenance of knowledge, measured and monitored by archives, that services an enlightened research culture and defines the literacies of expertise. Coherences between knowledge, self and society mobilised through memory, history and the archive are crucial to modern understandings of disciplinarity and education.

The connections between enlightenment, the liberal subject and the universal human forged in the curatorial efforts of the archive function to network authority into the fabric of knowing by fusing records with reality.

> *Modern national archives ... only gradually emerged after the French Revolution, but administrators and officials have kept and stored records, legal documents, privileges and decrees in archives since antiquity and within the Holy Roman Empire such older records remained a central part of the existing legal order. During the 17th century, this legal interest resulted in several so-called 'wars over documents' and prompted the development of new critical tools for the evaluation of manuscripts and detection of forgeries.*[16]

The archive rigorously defines, shapes and regulates a remembering/forgetting dyad. It is to re-tread familiar archival arguments (namely those of Derrida and Foucault) to affirm that archives are structuring systems that selectively assemble particular items, materials and documents for inclusion and exclusion. Equity is not a matter of simply affirming the inclusion of different perspectives, partial memories and the experiences of women, the working class, the colonised and the dispossessed as part of a larger social shift towards diversity and inclusion, but rather to acknowledge the ways in which archives are situated within a struggle over knowledge. How memory is conjured and contained, what is forgotten and framed – these are enacted in archival interactions. The archive is an ambiguous, mobile and evolving amoeba of documents, ideas, experiences and understandings. When this moves into a digitised environment fluidities, fragments and filaments reign. The boundaries between documents, classifications and catalogues begin to corrode as researchers can jump across texts and align perverse relationships in odd juxtapositions[17] – deconstructing the careful authority of the curator in assigning classifications thrashed out in 'document wars' and in service to a universal liberal subjectivity of progress, remembering, and development. History is recoded in these moments. Time is reconceptualised. Space is opened up for other ways of thinking and being. What is *not* recorded in the archive becomes as important as what *is* there and the decisions that landed those documents on the shelves or in the data. How we understand significance – of events, people, moments and memories – reiterates and rewrites itself.

> *Event and archive thus cannot be separated but have to be interrelationally positioned, something that is particularly evident in the current age of new archival monopolies such as Google, Facebook, YouTube, Twitter, or Tumblr which, in contradistinction to traditional archives, seem to operate less in a gate-keeping, exclusionary fashion, but exert the 'archival violence' on which Derrida has so much to say, through archiving itself as a default mode.*[18]

There is no need for gatekeepers online. Everything can be gathered, digitised and stored. The user determines what is to be known at the moment of retrieval. This does not democratise knowledge or inherently open up potentialities for forgotten knowledges. Instead, struggles over the cohesions between indexing, cataloguing and consciousness emerge. How the information is organised and catalogued becomes paramount. Hyperlinking is the currency of contemporary curation on social media. It editorialises the 'events', moments or memories of people's lives. It disjoins a moment out of the stream of the ordinary and marks it as unusual, separate and unique. On social media, people's profiles are crafted and constructed as are the snippets of their lives that they present as a curated public.[19] They are not archivists or curators as such but rather editors who cut and paste particularities of the ordinary to make banality exceptional. Managing a profile is to make all moments into 'events' – making them special and relevant. This has been in the evolving consciousness since 11 September 2001 and the global broadcast of the terrorist tragedy in New York, colliding global grief with 'nervous states'[20] within a risk-averse society and the currency of emotions, experiences and opinions deployed to make sense of contemporary zombified politics and displacement of the self in casino capitalism. The desire for 'the event' – for something to 'happen' as an arbiter and contrast to the mundanities of capitalism – is aped in the clever crafting of ordinary encounters and experiences on Facebook profiles and Instagram photos. Yet, these events are always lacking and must be reiterated and recycled in order to make meaning where emptiness reigns.

The desire is not for *an* event but for *the Event* that will reshape meaning – that might enable us to break free from capitalism. In Badiou's configuration, 'the event represents a radical, aleatory break with the norms governing a situation and the truth that it uncovers forces a transformation in the hierarchical ordering of that situation'.[21] This Event alters consciousness and brings a new awareness into being so that nothing can be the same again. This is not just because something has 'happened' or that it might have been 'traumatic' or terrorising, rather that it has created a rupture in thinking, being and doing and enters into the historical narrative as new meaning. Badiou affirms 'there are no natural events, nor are there neutral events',[22] they are potently disruptive and critically disobedient. The Event fundamentally 'belongs to conceptual construction'[23] where a *'traumatic intrusion of something New which remains unacceptable for the predominant view'*[24] asserts itself as a cascading collapse of multiples, spilling into a coherence of irrationalities and inconsistencies that find presence in what Badiou calls 'the void' which is 'non-one and unsubstantial'[25] – the place were all being and existence is conjured and cohered. Badiou argues that the French Revolution was such an Event. He argues that the multiple cohered into a singular – the many conflicts, interstices and interventions of the Revolution now fuse into one 'presentation' – *The* French Revolution.

> *Of the French Revolution as event it must be said that it both presents the infinite multiple of the sequence of facts situated between 1789 and 1794, and, moreover, that it presents itself as an immanent résumé and one-mark of its own multiple. The Revolution, even if it is interpreted as being such by historical retroaction, is no less, in itself, supernumerary to the sole numbering of the terms of its site, despite it presenting such a numbering. The event is thus clearly the multiple which both presents its entire site, and, by means of the pure signifier of itself immanent to its own multiple, manages to present the presentation itself, that is, the one of the infinite multiple that it is.*[26]

The struggle over the 'event' – indeed whether it exists, how it is being conjured, how it might be understood and rendered in historical memory, is seductive in the current consciousness of crisis and disaster. Our awareness of the potential evental was crystalized on 11 September 2001, when the Twin Towers collapsed. This was not an event in Badiou's definition. It served ultimately to *extend* rather than transform the meanings of neoliberalism, accelerated capitalism, violence, war and the real. Nevertheless, this shared experience, communicated through different representational structures, signifiers and symbols, media sites, critical analysis, photographs, documentaries and films created a superfluity. This was a global moment, and it spilled beyond its fragment. This 'global accident' conjures structures where 'the event is attached, to the place, to the point, in which the historicity of the situation is concentrated.'[27] 9/11 had all the ingredients of an Event, but its meanings were contained and constrained by established narratives. However, it does provide core markers for how evental moments appear. All the contestations and conflicts of meaning are brought to bear in the moment of the Twin Towers crash – the excessive site, the 'supre-sensible dimension which strikes us like lightning',[28] overburdened with possibilities so that 'the evental' possibility is the only sense-making strategy available. The authority and 'exceptionalism' of the United States crafted an unpredictable nexus in the hubris of political leaders and the internalised 'unforeseeability' of US vulnerability and terrorist rage. At New York City, 'the event ... evade[s] every calculus of prediction'[29] and it is with similar incredulity the election of Donald Trump and the Brexit decision are seen as potentially evental because they were 'incommensurable with all forms of knowledge operative within the situation'.[30] No memory, archive or education can adequately contain or represent the event because it is a 'pure ... happening'.[31] Resilience cannot anticipate or contain the event. Literacy changes because new ways of interpreting, understanding and knowing must emerge at the moment of the event. Education can prepare us, even if it cannot predict it, but new knowledge must emerge after, to account for the shift in possibilities. Therefore, the shocks of 9/11, the election of Donald Trump and the Brexit result present eruptions, but are not Events. The flows of the disintermediated digitised environment offer up the fluidities and flexibilities for evental potentialities to emerge, but their cohesion into events is unpredictable and only possible.

Such tremulous potentialities emerge among social media networks. The use of the Twitter tools, hashtags, retweeting (or via), and @, are a form of broadcasting for current happenings within the affordances of the Twitter platform where users 'amplify other users' voice'[32] by aggregating and layering interactions, responses and engagements. It is a multilayered universe where there are 'different levels of communication and media practices: from background, always on, "mundane and phatic" posting, to sudden shifts in vocabulary, topic, tone, and targets when important news enters the Twittersphere'.[33] This experience is not consistent among users, whose own profile constructs and interactive repertoire shape and alter the way in which the Twitter 'stream' is experienced. This 'stream' is dominated by the use of the hashtag (#) which heavily renders and accounts for Twitter's evental as well as temporal nature.

Twitter functions as a 'host of sensors for events as they happen'.[34] Tweets track events with initial interactions usually being informational in nature, followed by reactions, and then engagements between people assessing the consequences of the event. In this latter stage, the inadequacies of Twitter manifest as the inability of the short form to hold, maintain and sustain more complex conversations about the events are revealed. It is at this insecure moment that the crowd-sourced syllabus can emerge to widen the debate. As the potentialities of the event conjure, bubble and pervade in digitised form, its transition into a syllabus – a way of organising the ephemeralities of the unfolding – forces 'the situation to confront the traumatic void which is its deepest, most "repressed" truth'.[35] The hashtag functions to aggregate these interactions into an evolving and fluid archive that logs the networked nature of knowledge emerging and forming during these potentially evental engagements. The hashtag operates as a networked index and changes the way in which knowledge is catalogued, accessed and distributed, offering up contestable truths. Where once the assignation of a keyword was enacted by trained librarians and archival personnel who assessed texts and imbued an historical authority on the information contained within documents, it is now created in an 'interactive temporality'[36] of the flows and arcs of user-generated tweets. These mobilities are teasing out the potentials enfolded in 'events'. When the Twittersphere cannot constrain the potentials and possibilities of the unfolding happenings, the syllabus is created to permit knowing to spill over into an appendix that navigates the truths that cannot be confronted. The librarian or archival gatekeeper that mediated an 'ideal of universal knowledge'[37] which 'requires absolute distance between the knower and the known'[38] is diminished in these relationships. The hashtag and Twitter more generally permits a corrosion of these distinctions. It has collapsed the distance between the knower and the known. It has also dislodged the expert. The softening of gatekeeper responsibilities and acceleration of hyperlinked networked interactions allow different voices to be heard and to be bearers of the truths that the Event confronts.

The hashtag operationalises a stream as an eventual process of becoming – a space where issues, ideas, concepts and happenings coincide and merge, sliding in and out of importance according to the moment – or what has been called 'Twitter time' – 'a specific instance of network time, but itself only a "pattern of pace" from which further temporalities are instantiated'.[39] According to Pond this is not 'a single instance of Twitter time, but ... an artificial declaration of temporal unity'.[40] This space of and for becoming is where the eventual nature of a happening is negotiated. As such, it is not 'stream density' or trending topics that decides something might be an 'event' but the way in which the hashtag enters, interfaces and dialogues with virtual and analogue spaces that brings the potentialities of multiples together. The crowd-sourced syllabus as an outcome of this process provides a cache for eventual discussions and debates. The hashtag transforms into an archive when it logs and gathers together informal and formal knowledges, expert and popular knowledges offering a multitude of experiences, negotiations and inferences. Informally or formally, the crowd is leveraged to cohere in a specific space and time facilitated by the hashtag. In these spaces of struggle over meaning, the hashtag creates tension between the official narratives of a 'happening' and the non-elites or ordinary people who respond, intervene and interact in news events as they unfold, and then commentators, critics and scholars who offer up contestable truths. The crowd may include experts and novices, empowered and disempowered who cohere, connect and communicate in these moments. Potentials and possibilities are funnelled through the hashtag and present multiple temporalities within the accelerated unfolding in which it communicates.

In these aggregations of moments, crowd-sourcing emerges as a way of organising experience, managing information and presenting possibilities for knowledge. The crowd-sourced syllabus emerges from a hashtag that is operationalised by an individual or organisation in order to develop and expand the stream density into a literacy for processing, perceiving and prevailing upon a potentially evental moment by offering up difficult truths. For the hashtag syllabus in its complex crowd-sourcing, a negotiation over an event is taking place. This is unfolding in the aggregation of literacies that are being networked to draw together ways of knowing and understanding that redefine the relationship between the known and the knower. The crowd-sourced syllabus opens up the void and reveals the multiples (of experiences, knowledges and literacies) that contest for coherence – the struggle over how or if the event will enter into being 'evental'. What knowledges circulate and how these might be arranged to offer an alternative reading of a 'happening' is offered in the crowd-sourced syllabus. Possibilities are struggled over. What is considered an 'event' is questioned as is whether it might even be an 'event' at all. This is also a space of remembering and forgetting. In the density of the stream, old knowledges can be conjured via the crowd which is disobedient and often deviant. Knowledges forgotten and suppressed or hidden in the official archive are centralised. Crowd-sourcing calls upon obscured, masked and forgotten knowledges to be accountable alongside the contemporary and new. Because 'the crowd' is made up of an unpredictable diversity and is conjured into existence around the emergence of a potential event, the knowledges it calls upon, deploys and distributes are contingent, unlocked and diverse. This complexity must be organised by the hashtag which allows tweets to aggregate. Twitter creates the space for a 'crowd-sourced specialist "awareness system"'[41] to conjure contested truths. There is a negotiation of public discourse in these moments. A gatekeeper, or multiple gatekeepers, according to interest or desire, can organise and frame the resources contributed by the crowd – placing order and context around the situatedness of these resources. In the case studies in this book, the gatekeepers are mostly educators with a desire to enact an engaged and reflexive pedagogy and who actively call upon the crowd to harvest diverse, hidden and unspoken resources related to the narratives of the dispossessed. The disintermediated nature of the crowd-sourced syllabus, conjured via the hashtag and organically archived in the stream, presents the potential for the double refusal by conjuring contested and repressed truths to open space for The Event.

A crowd-sourced syllabus is an output of a complex navigational and negotiable situation where struggles over the 'ever-present possibility of the event'[42] is realised. Current resources and educational repertoires are acknowledged as inadequate to understand events and how 'the real' is contested. Instead, the hashtag is leveraged as an evolving arena where contestability means that debate is opened rather than closed. In this opening, meaning is unsettled as is significance, self and power. How we understand the events, how those moments are contextualised and recoded become mobile and unsettled and where the potential for the double refusal appears. Via the hashtag, resources that reject and defamiliarize the official narratives of law and order that conjure the use of violence against insurrectionary identities are questioned. A resistance is presented in #BlackLivesMatter, #MeToo, #standwithstandingrock. Such resistances are part of the 'affective publics' and communal consciousness of the Arab Spring movement and Occupy Wall Street #ows. However, in crafting a syllabus for teaching and learning curated from the crowd and its potentialities and possibilities for understanding moments, events and happenings, refusal is called forth, assessed and understood. This two-way process, of cultivating refusal, but also opening up multiple ways of remembering, processing and enacting the knowledge gathered means that rebellion is not an end point. Ways of moving into affective knowledges that question and reveal the processes of domination and enable radical praxis are present. The evolving, living nature of the hashtag and the archive it creates means potentials are opened and ways towards an educated hope are mapped. A crowd-sourced syllabus is a refusal of a functional education for workplace readiness. It is a refusal of static resistance. It is also a refusal to dominate by calling forth the knowledges needed to understand 'the real', the moment, the event. The case studies that follow were all conjured at and through specific 'moments': happenings that arced together historical crises and conflicts into cataclysmic contestation. The struggle to understand if these moments were, or would become, Events, manifested in the creation of crowd-sourced syllabi that deployed reading lists, film, photographs, maps and archival complexities of forgotten and remembered items to radically contextualise the meanings emerging in and via these events. The potential of teaching and learning is reclaimed via the hashtag for an interrogation of 'the real' that opens the possibility for an educated hope where the double refusal lingers.

NOTES

1. Siva Vaidhyanathan, *The Googlization of Everything: And Why We Should Worry* (Berkley: The University of California Press, 2011), 1.
2. Matteo Pasquinelli, "Google's PageRank Algorithm: A Diagram of the Cognitive Capitalism and the Rentier of the Common Intellect," in *Deep Search: The Politics of Search Beyond Google*, eds. Konrad Becker and Felix Stadler (London: Transaction Publishers, 2009), 155.

3. Pasquinelli, "Google's PageRank Algorithm," 155.
4. Tara Brabazon, *The University of Google: Education in the (Post) Information Age* (London: Routledge, 2016).
5. Brabazon, The University of Google, 16–17.
6. Tara Brabazon, "5 Minutes to Hell. Time to Tell the Truth: The Disintermediated Doctoral Student," *Fast Capitalism* 14, i. 1, (2017): 92, doi: 10.32855/fcapital.201701.014.
7. Brabazon, "5 Minutes to Hell," 92.
8. George P. Landow, *Hypertext 3.0: Critical Theory and New Media in the Era of Globalization* (Maryland: The Johns Hopkins University Press, 2006), 196.
9. It is important to note that ideas are not formed in linear and grounded ways but may be activated along unpredictable and insightful inspirational networks. See Mihaly Csikszentmihalyi, *Flow: The Psychology of Optimal Experience* (New York: Harper Perennial, 1990).
10. Landow, Hypertext 3.0, 113.
11. Landow, Hypertext 3.0, 117.
12. Mike Featherstone, "Archive," *Theory, Culture and Society* 23, no. 2–3, (2006): 593, https://doi.org/10.1177/0263276406023002106.
13. Boris Jardine and Matthew Drage, "The Total Archive: Data, Subjectivity, Universality," *History of the Human Sciences* 31, no. 5, (2018): 5, https://doi.org/10.1177/0952695118820806.
14. Jardine and Drage, "The Total Archive," 8.
15. Sheenagh Pietrobruno, "YouTube and the Social Archiving of Intangible Heritage," *New Media and Society* 15, no. 8, (2013): 1261, https://doi.org/10.1177/1461444812469598.
16. Kasper Risbjerg Eskildsen, "Inventing the Archive: Testimony and Virtue in Modern Historiography," *History of the Human Sciences* 26, no. 4, (2013): 13, https://doi.org/10.1177/0952695113496094.
17. Featherstone, "Archive," 595.
18. Basel Abbas and Ruanne Abou-Rahme (in conversation with Tom Holert), "The Archival Multitude," *Journal of Visual Culture* 12, no. 3, (2013), 346, https://doi.org/10.1177/1470412913502031.
19. See Mikaela Pitcan, Alice E. Marwick, and danah boyd, "Performing a Vanilla Self: Respectability Politics, Social Class, and the Digitised World," *Journal of Computer Mediated Communication* 23, (2018): 163–179, https://doi.org/10.1093/jcmc/zmy008.
20. William Davies, *Nervous States: How Feelings Took Over the World* (London: Penguin, 2018).
21. Colin Wright, "Event or Exception?: Disentangling Badiou from Schmitt, or, Towards a Politics of the Void," *Theory and Event* 11, i. 2, (2008), https://muse.jhu.edu/article/240327, Project Muse.
22. Alain Badiou, *Being and Event* (London: Continuum, 2006), 178.
23. Badiou, Being and Event, 178.
24. Slavoj Žižek, *Event*, (London: Penguin, 2014), 78.
25. Badiou, Being and Event, 56.
26. Badiou, Being and Event, 180.
27. Badiou, Being and Event, 179.
28. Žižek, Event, 80.

29. Wright, "Event or Exception?"
30. Wright, "Event or Exception?"
31. Wright, "Event or Exception?"
32. Stefania Vicari, "Twitter and Non-Elites: Interpreting Power Dynamics in the Life Story of the (#)BRCA Twitter Stream," *Social Media and Society* (July – September 2017): 3 https://doi.org/10.1177/2056305117733224.
33. Vicari, "Twitter and Non-Elites," 2.
34. Mahmud Hasan, Mehmet A. Orgun, and Rolf Schwitter, "A Survey on Real-Time Event Detection from the Twitter Data Stream," *Journal of Information Science* 44, no. 4, (2018): 443, https://doi.org/10.1177/0165551517698564.
35. Wright, "Event or Exception?"
36. Philip Pond, "Twitter Time: A Temporal Analysis of Tweet Streams During Televised Political Debate," *Television and New Media* 17, no. 2, (2016): 154, https://doi.org/10.1177/1527476415616190.
37. Jardine and Drage, "The Total Archive," 16.
38. Jardine and Drage, "The Total Archive," 16.
39. Pond, "Twitter Time," 144.
40. Pond, "Twitter Time," 144.
41. Vicari, "Twitter and Non-Elites," 12.
42. Wright, "Event or Exception?"

4

#FERGUSONSYLLABUS

That morning in 2012, during my first year of teaching, a timid 15-year-old Black male student, whose name coincidentally was also Trayvon, raised a question to me. He asked, 'Mr J., have you heard about the shooting of Trayvon Martin?' With a look of confusion, I replied, 'No, I haven't'. Trayvon proceeded to explain the story of Trayvon Martin's murder and how the neighbourhood watchman racially profiled and physically abused him.

As Trayvon continued to share the story about Trayvon Martin, a few students gave head nods of affirmation while echoes of 'yeah, I heard about that' permeated the room. Aaron, a Black male teenager, yelled, 'Why did that watchman do him like that?' While I facilitated the critical conversation, I simultaneously searched the web for a news media clip that would help explain the racial incident. In a space of contestation, I witnessed my 14- and 15-year-old Black students wrestling with the misperceptions, stereotypes, and racial violence that are inflicted upon Black lives.[1]

This anecdote serves as a crucial reminder that classrooms are not separate from the world. It also demonstrates how responsive teachers are increasingly required to be in the age of social media where events unfold at speed. Educators must deploy a miscellany of skills to adapt to the tendrils of changeability that slide inside and outside of the classroom. Educators know that conjuring effective tools instantaneously on the web is fraught with complexity. They must fact-check and assess resources for not only truth but also appropriateness. They must deploy a high level of digital media literacy in order to be responsive in classroom settings when such events unfold. It is within this mobile framework that the hashtag #FergusonSyllabus was created, two years after Trayvon Martin was killed, so that teachers could have ready on-hand materials and resources that could immediately be applied as events unfolded in Ferguson.

Michael Brown Jr.'s death was yet another in the history of police violence. In 2012 Trayvon Martin's death, though not by a police officer but by private citizen George Zimmerman, stimulated the outpouring of resistance, rebellion and anger that would percolate into #BlackLivesMatter. This hashtag was created as a point of activism, and as a ballast against which critique and radical intervention into social conditions could be launched. Unlike the outcome at Ferguson, #BlackLivesMatter is not a specific call for resources in a crowd-sourced syllabus.[2] #BlackLivesMatter is a social movement that deploys syllabi as one component of its wider resistance project. Importantly, the hashtag functions as an anchor, constructing a central node around which many and varied spokes and hubs form, expand and intersect for the many projects and resources deploying, mobilising and aggregating #BlackLivesMatter moments.

#BlackLivesMatter was initiated by three women – Patrisse Cullors, Alicia Garza and Opal Tometi. In the wake of the acquittal of George Zimmerman, Garza tweeted 'black people. I love you. I love us. Our lives matter'[3] to which Cullors added 'declaration: black bodies will no longer be sacrificed for the rest of the world's enlightenment. i am done. trayvon, you are loved infinitely. #blacklivesmatter'.[4] These women are activists who come from a deep heritage of resistance. The Black Lives Matter movement has a set of guiding principles[5] but no centralised power structure, making it highly responsive and flexible. It leverages the hashtag to facilitate this flexibility to harness and aggregate resources along multiple tangents of use. In mapping the origins and (evolving) outcomes of the movement, there is a clear necessity to contextualise the hashtag as only one element of a considered and complex social intervention that aims to have real-world impact on a variety of fronts. Alicia Garza has celebrated 'moving the hashtag from social media to the streets'[6] as an important diversification of its political and social impact. It is important to understand #BlackLivesMatter as aiming to have impact beyond social media with education and learning infrastructures just one part of a concerted and coordinated activist effort.

The creation of the #FergusonSyllabus hashtag by Marcia Chatelain was to gather resources to help her teach in an immediate response to the trauma of Michael Brown Jr.'s death and the public outcry manifesting in civil disobedience in Ferguson. While it is part of an activist repertoire, it is not its primary objective. Rather, its aim is to hack pedagogy. Chatelain put out the call on Twitter for contributions of readings and resources that could help teachers and students make sense of unfolding events – to provide a repertoire of knowing that could be deployed within the classroom.

> *I wanted other educators to think about how painful the introduction to a new school year would be for this town. I hoped to challenge my colleagues on campuses across the country to devote the first day of classes to a conversation about Ferguson.*
>
> *What emerged was a small call for community across the sometimes impersonal and expansive digital world. I asked professors who used Twitter to talk about Ferguson and to use #FergusonSyllabus to recommend texts, collaborate on conversation starters, and inspire dialogue about some aspect of the Ferguson crisis. Slowly high school teachers, early education specialists, guidance counselors, and middle-school instructors wanted ideas too.*[7]

While #FergusonSyllabus can be broadly situated within the purview of #BlackLivesMatter, it holds a different intent and deploys the hashtag more precisely. #FergusonSyllabus aims at drawing together and revealing the multiples and possibilities present in the Ferguson moment to begin the sense-making process. The hashtag forms a fulcrum to allow the aggregation of materials, potentials and possibilities – for multiples to replicate, shift and change, for many experiences, histories, herstories, complexities and truths to interface and weave a way to knowing. The hashtag provided the real-time response and the tentacles of outreach into the crowd to source strategies for critically conscious and empathetic learning to occur. These materials were conjured because the current pedagogies were inadequate to the needs of processing, pondering and parsing what was happening in Ferguson. Instructors needed responsive, difficult and perhaps even unsanctioned materials to begin the hard work of unpacking the witnessed events.

Ferguson offered a fulcrum. It makes little sense that this shooting provided a catalyst for social upheaval. A wider context needed to be understood why Michael Brown Jr.'s murder created a catalyst for refusal to spill over into radical rejection of the dominant order in Ferguson. Data on fatal police shootings of citizens show consistency of incidents. 'Recent data from the UCR [Uniform Crime Report] and NVSS [National Vital Statistics System] have shown that police killings of citizens have remained relatively stable over the past 10 years [2007–2017]'.[8] These killings are racialised; '37% of unarmed people killed by police were Black in 2015 despite Black people being only

13% of the population in the United States'.[9] The killing of Michael Brown Jr. was not an 'environmental jolt', but yet another act in a long line of state-sanctioned violence against black bodies in the United States. The outrage at Ferguson erupted not just because it was the first major incident involving white police and a black victim post Trayvon Martin and the creation of #BlackLivesMatter. It was not only due to the incendiary and sensationalist media fodder of Michael Brown Jr.'s body laying dead in the street for up to four hours past the critical incident. Nor was it the mass protests bubbling into public view that later resulted in the calling of SWAT to attendance. It was the context in which these events were unfolding, most importantly, the election of Barack Obama to the United States presidency and the corroding perceptions of a post-race America unfolding before the public's eyes.

As the first (self-identifying) black man elected to the presidency of the United States of America Barack Obama marked a turning point in the United States consciousness. The racial tensions that had so stricken the nation in the long struggle to deliver real and effective civil rights since the upheavals of the 1960s, and the tensions plaguing crime narratives around black incarceration in the 1980s, seemed to ease away in the soothing balm of Obama's rhetoric. Before the percolation of his placating oratory Obama was considered 'a previously marginal candidate who was thought to have little chance of winning the presidency'.[10] A master rhetorician, Obama was able to bolster support through the nuanced narratives he was able to weave in his speeches, carefully walking between the interests of diverse constituents. The 'Yes, we can' slogan is indicative of the positive togetherness Obama advocated. Via the dualism of hope and empathy he sought to craft a post-race America. Obama spoke to healing the nation and creating a cohesive and strong community. He deployed emotion to generate connections between constituents and soothe their anxieties about the future. He achieved this by conjuring the past and acknowledging the dualities and binaries percolating through contentious experiences, thereby pacifying both black and white voters, liberals and conservatives.

Obama is not the first politician to conjure empathy in his campaign. Pedwell[11] has acknowledged Bill Clinton using the phrase 'I feel your pain' along with the Republican establishment's 'compassionate conservatism' as alternate and earlier versions of this intention. Obama's deployment of hope is particular and his '"audacity of hope" rhetoric is … a revised and updated version of Jackson's "keep hope alive" slogan'.[12] Obama's success is not only in his dexterity with language and personability, but that he carefully integrates and obfuscates neoliberal ideologies. The empathetic and caring individual in Obama's conjuring is an 'ideal neoliberal citizen'[13] who is a 'self-managing and self-enterprising individual'[14] able to operate optimally – physically and emotionally – within the neoliberal order. This individual is resilient, compassionate and caring, but within a framework that operates to wipe away and radically reimagine the past. The 'neoliberal visions of social justice'[15] evoked by Obama 'evacuate "past" legacies of oppression and inequality to envision an "empathic" market society that transcend (but in reality re-entrenches) social divisions'.[16] These imaginings are in order to facilitate a stable, forward-looking capitalist economic outlook uninterrupted by racial and other tensions. The hope being conjured is sedate and unoffensive.

> *the affective narrative of hope and empathy that was so seductive to so many throughout Obama's election campaign has – from the arena of health care reform to the war in Iraq, to the Wall Street bailout – led not to a radical 'break with current political history' but, rather, to political inertia, with Obama promoting 'quasi-Republican economic and foreign policy norms'.[17]*

The hopeful trope is slippery, enabling the assignation of variable and volatile meanings. It is seductive and forward-looking, assisting in a redirection of the past towards better opportunities in which 'hope could be described as a "wish orientation" towards future objects or possibilities which are perceived as necessary, good or pleasurable but which are not yet present'.[18] Obama conjured an idealised hope that was always in becoming. He alluded to the character of the American nation and the tenacity of its citizens, thereby denying the atomisation of difference along racial lines. Obama's 'A More Perfect Union' speech is considered by many a crucial turning point early in his campaign for presidency where this ability to align and cohere hope with normative neoliberalism could be tracked. Obama's personal Pastor Jeremiah Wright had made a series of 'controversial' statements that implicated Obama by his close association.[19] It stood to inflame tensions about race, bigotry and white privilege. Obama used the speech to distance himself from Wright without confronting his black voting supporter base, hailing other marginalised groups, while also placating white voters. He achieved this by evoking liminality, speaking to experiences of dispossession while mobilising a hopeful imagining of the future in which things 'could' be better. He did not apportion blame and render painful pasts but rather aligned the interests of different groups and presented them in a common imagining of the American community.

> *For the African-American community, that path means embracing the burdens of our past without becoming victims of our past. It*

> means continuing to insist on a full measure of justice in every aspect of American life. But it also means binding our particular grievances, for better health care and better schools and better jobs, to the larger aspirations of all Americans – the white woman struggling to break the glass ceiling, the white man who's been laid off, the immigrant trying to feed his family. And it means also taking full responsibility for our own lives – by demanding more from our fathers, and spending more time with our children, and reading to them, and teaching them that while they may face challenges and discrimination in their own lives, they must never succumb to despair or cynicism. They must always believe – They must always believe that they can write their own destiny.[20]

Rather than providing a fulcrum around which issues of race could be discussed and aired, Obama pasted over racial distinctions and provided a neatly tailored package of otherness which asserted a post-racial America where colour blindness reigned. Voting for Obama was a sort of affirmation of being 'not racist'. He was the embodiment of the 'post-racial age' that citizens had hoped existed. By affirming his heritage from his 'Kenyan father and white mother' Obama hailed an integrated and tolerant community. Importantly, Obama gave the white community permission to remain 'wilfully ignorant' about racism, and while he acknowledged the experiences of black people and other minorities, did not give them full voice. The deployment of 'hope' permitted a liminality to emerge during Obama's presidency where the permanent delay and displacement of social justice existed in this in-between space, never quite arriving. Ferguson became the pivotal moment for hope at the end of the Obama presidency. It was the nexus at which hope's potentials and problems cascaded. It was the moment where hoping was no longer enough and the pasts which were to be either forgotten in exchange for economic success, or remembered in militant and angry terms were mediated by the hashtag. Ferguson was a potential 'event' where 'repressed truths' erupted in refusal.

Hope became a space for struggle. Deray McKesson writes about the 'work' of hope, reflecting upon the fear, strength and uncertainty of the activism he chose at Ferguson. He argues that hope is something hard won. Hope resides in optimism and is an imperfect antidote to the contemporary despair and nihilism we currently live with in accelerated capitalism. This is not to assert false platitudes about remaining positive and wishing for a better world – or obfuscating political positions like Obama did. McKesson is clear about the action that is needed to cultivate, cajole and create hopeful opportunities. It is a process of acknowledging that different hierarchies of hope exist, and that in order for hope to become an active and transformative experience requires work. It is in this space where transcendence might be achieved. For McKesson hope is not just 'wishful' thinking. He argues that 'faith is the belief that certain outcomes *will* happen and hope is the belief that certain outcomes *can* happen'.[21] In order for hope to be productive it must work to present potentials. Ferguson was the moment when hope went from wishing that something will happen to asserting that something *could* happen and acknowledging that refusal is needed for this transformation. It was a potential 'event' that amplified uncomfortable truths and collisions of radical meanings. The deployment of the #FergusonSyllabus was a call to 'educated hope' that could make sense of the eruption at Ferguson and how it could reform the way the everyday 'real' was understood by citizens.

The creation of the Ferguson syllabus hashtag brings together resources that frame hope within history – hope that has a reason, an outcome, a purpose, a heritage and a function – transforming it into educated hope. Educated hope recentralises education to politics. An educated hope is about undermining oppression and bringing about productive change located in a disobedient rendering of justice and critical consciousness. It involves 'making the political more pedagogical'.[22] By accessing the 'everyday real' and codifying pedagogies in the present, an unfurling of the purposes of power can filter through strategies of radical thinking.

> *Making the political more pedagogical in this instance suggests producing modes of knowledge and social practices that not only affirm oppositional cultural work and pedagogical practices but also offer opportunities to mobilize instances of collective outrage coupled with direct mass action, against a ruthless casino capitalism and an emerging fascist politics. Such mobilization must oppose the glaring material inequities and the growing cynical belief that democracy and capitalism are synonymous.*[23]

The crowd-sourced syllabus that emerged out of the events at Ferguson deploys educated hope as a method for enabling the double refusal. That double refusal leads to collective outrage and transformation. McKesson argues that 'hope is the precursor to strategy'[24] and that it 'powers our vision of what role we must play in bringing about a desired goal'.[25] In this space the potentialities of the event percolate in anticipation of reconfiguration. The work of hope is present in protest and resistance, not just against the rise of the right or against neoliberalism or oppression, but in crafting the future that is desired – one where the double refusal opens repressed truths.

McKesson uses his experiences at Ferguson to show how the political can be pedagogical. He shows how both the presence and absence of data offers spaces for those in power to compose their own narratives, truths and realities. Until Ferguson, the United States government did not collect data on police shootings. The FBI is supposed to gather this data, but the Supplementary Homicide Report relies on self-reported data, which is unreliable. The work of McKesson and the data gathering team at Ferguson found 'that police kill twelve hundred people each year in America' and that the bulk of these killings are of black people.

> In Baltimore, we found that every person killed by a police officer for as far back as our database went, to 2014, was a black man. In Cleveland, we showed that everyone killed since 2012, all ten people, were black, and seven were unarmed. We found that St. Louis has by far the highest rate of police violence in the country. Black men in St. Louis are killed by police at a rate twice as high as the US murder rate.[26]

The scale of the data revealed by McKesson and the Ferguson research team debunks the myths crafted by police and authorities about police killings of black people, namely that they are connected to high crime, high poverty confluences. The data showed that such connections were false and that there is an infrastructure of police violence percolating throughout these communities where 'police were choosing to be violent regardless'.[27] The shaping of the violence narrative is controlled by police and authorities when there is a lack of language in which to speak of these contested spaces. When the language is colonised by power, hope remains a wishing trope. In the deployment of the syllabus that hope shifts to a productive and proactive struggle with repressed truth and the opening of a double refusal in the articulation of the event. Language frames and defines the ways in which concepts and contexts are deployed, offering a space from which to act – an actionable and educated hope that tracks a pathway from understanding into the real.

The crowd-sourced syllabus is a gathering of resources about the past, in the present, for a future that has not arrived yet. How one uses those resources and how one crafts the future is contestable, struggled over and debated. Tracks into the past must be uncovered, retrodden and their truths harvested to be able to action in the present the politics, justice and freedoms we want. Crafting the language with which to speak is the first step. #FergusonSyllabus was the tool through which resources could be gathered to respond in real time to the changing and shifting reality of Ferguson and the United States more broadly. In this acceleration, the narrative could be mapped and tracked, resources offered to make sense of and move with the evolving eventual situation, rather than silence being filled with authoritative or official narratives that do not add complexity or reify diversity, but are instead seeking to re-establish order, contain and curtail disruption and assert authoritative structures that are oppressive, standardised and narrow.

The #FergusonSyllabus has stimulated compilations of materials from the resources offered. Chatelain presented an edited summary for 'a community of teachers, academics, community leaders and parents'[28] in *The Atlantic* in August 2014. Compiled directly from the #FergusonSyllabus contributions, Chatelain sorted it into 13 sections: Teaching about Race and Ferguson; African-American History/Civil Rights in the United States; Children's Books; Community Organizing, Leadership, Activism; Educational Issues; Film; Media Studies and Journalism; Music; Other Educational Hashtags on Twitter; Personal Reflections; Poetry; Policing; and Race and Violence in America. Materials include Ted Talks, essays by James Baldwin, blogs, autobiographies, writing by Martin Luther King Jr, speeches, *Do the Right Thing*, photographs, music by Lauren Hill, entries by a diversity of scholars and journalists.

In the gathering of perspectives and viewpoints, histories and experiences, space is opened for thinking, critiquing and processing. These are the spaces of and for hope – where alternatives can be visualised and action mobilised. These are spaces where a double refusal can be imagined – not just resistance or a refusal to be dominated, but a moving of consciousness into a space where domination can be rewritten into a refusal to dominate in actions, speaking and being. In the diversity of resources offered by this snapshot of the #FergusonSyllabus, an intersection of histories, experiences, truths, traces and tropes cohere to offer up educated hope and tools for unfolding and unfurling the temporalities of Twitter that interface with the tenacities of teaching and the labours of learning, moving into a future that can be conscious and caring.

The success of the #FergusonSyllabus served as a model for events emerging not quite a year after Michael Brown's murder. #CharlestonSyllabus was created in response to Dylan Roof's murder of nine people in the bible study group at Emanuel African Methodist Episcopal Church in Charleston South Carolina on 17 June 2015. Unlike the events at Ferguson, this was not a police action, but the work of a white supremacist invoking racial nationalism in his decision to murder black people. Like Ferguson, it was the acknowledgement that Roof was not an anomaly, that his actions were part of a long history of white supremacy in the United States and taking place against the backdrop of a supposed post-racial nation where the election of a black president had soothed the populace and marked the movement of the United States into racial maturity and social tolerance. Instead of reducing racism, the election of Obama had only masked its enduring legacy. Instead of allowing Roof's encoding of blackness to stand, the #CharlestonSyllabus was deployed in order to respond to his rendering of race, to resist, critique and deploy a diversity of tools and techniques to engage with race via the past in the present. The responsiveness of the syllabus enabled real-time activation of alternative narratives, complexity and diversity to be deployed in managing and mentoring student knowledge as they negotiated unfolding events. Contextualising Roof's actions was conjured as an urgent intervention into the official narratives that would determine how Charleston would be remembered and invoked in the future. In order to ensure space for the double refusal, the #CharlestonSyllabus conjured the repressed truths of white supremacism and deployed spaces in which to activate critical consciousness, craft an educated hope and pursue radical thinking.

The potency of the crowd-sourced syllabus, particularly as it emerges around issues of racial tension in the United States, has waned in the post-Obama period. In August 2017, nearly a year after the election of Donald Trump to the United States presidency white supremacists descended upon Charlottesville in Virginia to hold a 'Unite the Right' rally in protest of the removal of a statue of Confederate General Robert E. Lee from Emancipation Park near the University of Virginia. In the clash of protesters, a car was driven into the crowd of counter-protesters and a woman, Heather Heyer, was killed. While #Charlottesville and variants of this hashtag trended on Twitter, there was no emerging Charlottesville syllabus cascading in real time. Instead, a syllabus[29] emerged after the events unfolded by scholars seeking to contextualise and control the narratives surrounding it, but without the added intent of operationalising this knowledge inside the classrooms for students as a tool for making sense of an emergent situation. In the context of Trump's presidency, such racism was not unexpected. There is no longer a pretence of post-racism in Trump's America. The Charlottesville syllabus is not seeking space for the double refusal, sensing an opportunity to rethink and recode hopefulness through action, knowledge and interrogation. These truths are no longer repressed or simmering with bubbling potentiality of the event.

NOTES

1. Lamar L. Johnson, "Where Do We Go From Here?: Toward a Critical Race English Education," *Research in the Teaching of English* 53, no. 2, (2018): 103.
2. The Black Lives Matter syllabus is compiled by Frank Leon Roberts, a member of Faculty at New York University as part of the trove of resources,

ideas and items and movements under the #BlackLivesMatter mantle. The fully formed curriculum is a credit bearing course at the university's Gallatin School of Individualized Study entitled 'Black lives Matter: Race, Resistance, and Populist Protest'. It is one of hundreds of seminars offered at Gallatin in the Interdisciplinary Seminar component of the degree programme that allows students to responsively interpret and expand their understanding of events. There are many other similar syllabi at other Universities, notably Dartmouth College, for example, where the course (no longer being offered) was called '10 Weeks, 10+ Professors: #BlackLivesMatter', accessed January 30, 2020, https://news.dartmouth.edu/news/2015/02/dartmouth-offer-new-course-blacklivesmatter.

3. Patrisse Cullors, "Black Lives Matter: Not a Moment, But a Movement," accessed March 3, 2020, https://patrissecullors.com/black-lives-matter/.
4. Cullors, "Black Lives Matter."
5. Black Lives Matter, "What We Believe," accessed March 1, 2020, https://blacklivesmatter.com/what-we-believe/.
6. Alicia Garza, "Black Lives Matter," *The Feminist Wire*, October 7, 2014, https://www.thefeministwire.com/2014/10/blacklivesmatter-2/.
7. Marcia Chatelain, "Teaching the #FergusonSyllabus," *Dissent Magazine*, November 28, 2014, https://www.dissentmagazine.org/blog/teaching-ferguson-syllabus.
8. Bradley A. Campbell, Justin Nix, and Edward R. Maguire, "Is the Number of Citizens Fatally Shot by Police Increasing in the Post-Ferguson Era?" *Crime and Delinquency* 64, no. 3, (2017): 401, https://doi.org/10.1177/0011128716686343.
9. Mia Moody-Ramirez and Hazel Col, "Victim Blaming in Twitter Users' Framing of Eric Garner and Michael Brown," *Journal of Black Studies* 49, no. 4, (2018): 385, https://doi.org/10.1177/0021934718754312.
10. Carolyn Pedwell, "Economies of Empathy: Obama, Neoliberalism, and Social Justice," *Environment and Planning D: Society and Space* 30, (2012): 291, https://doi.org/10.1068/d22710.
11. Pedwell, "Economies of Empathy," 284.
12. Martell Teasley and David Ikard, "Barack Obama and the Politics of Race: The Myth of Postracism in America," *Journal of Black Studies* 40, no. 3, (2010): 417, https://doi.org/10.1177/0021934709352991.
13. Pedwell, "Economies of Empathy," 286.
14. Pedwell, "Economies of Empathy," 286.
15. Pedwell, "Economies of Empathy," 295.
16. Pedwell, "Economies of Empathy," 295.
17. Pedwell, "Economies of Empathy," 291.
18. Pedwell, "Economies of Empathy," 290.
19. See Clarence E. Walker and Gregory D. Smithers, *The Preacher and the Politician: Jeremiah Wright, Barack Obama, and Race in America* (Charlottesville: University of Virginia Press, 2009).
20. Barack Obama, *A More Perfect Union*, speech delivered March 18, 2008, Philadelphia PA, *American Rhetoric*, 9, https://www.americanrhetoric.com/speeches/PDFFiles/Barack%20Obama%20-%20More%20Perfect%20Union.pdf.

21. Deray Mckesson, *On the Other Side of freedom: The Case for Hope* (New York: Viking, 2018), 6.
22. Henry A. Giroux and Ourania Filippakou, "Critical Pedagogy in the Age of Authoritarianism: Challenges and Possibilities," *Revista Izquierdas* 49, (2020), 8.
23. Giroux and Filippakou, "Critical Pedagogy," 8.
24. Mckesson, *On the Other Side of Freedom*, 8.
25. Mckesson, *On the Other Side of Freedom*, 8.
26. Mckesson, *On the Other Side of Freedom*, 54.
27. Mckesson, *On the Other Side of Freedom*, 60.
28. Marcia Chatelain, "How to Teach Kids about What's Happening in Ferguson: A Crowdsourced Syllabus about Race, African American History, Civil Rights and Policing," *The Atlantic*, August 25, 2014, https://www.theatlantic.com/education/archive/2014/08/how-to-teach-kids-about-whats-happening-in-ferguson/379049/.
29. Chris Howard-Woods, Colin Laidley, and Maryam Omidi, eds., *Charlottesville: White Supremacy, Populism, and Resistance* (New York: Public Seminar Books, 2018).

5

#NEWFASCISMSYLLABUS

To the Editor:

> *Over the past year, scholars have curated a number of public syllabi and reading lists, most crowdsourced through social media, to provide historical context for understanding various contemporary events and phenomena. Many of these carefully thought-out efforts represent the best of academic public engagement, respect for scholarly diversity, and a commitment to social justice.*
>
> *On every count, the 'Trump Syllabus' (24 June 2016), published as part of* The Chronicle Review's *special issue on the 'phenomenon that is Donald Trump's presidential campaign', does not.*[1]

This letter to the editor of *The Chronicle of Higher Education* in the aftermath of their publication of a Trump syllabus criticises the neglect of Indigenous and Black scholars on the reading list.[2] The authors declare,

> The syllabus fails to include the works of scholars of color, thereby perpetuating the message that the only works worth reading in American political history are those written by white scholars.[3]

In their rush to leverage the new and emerging interest in online syllabi being created in the crises interrupting the political landscape, *The Chronicle Review* had hastily cobbled together a reading list with little consideration of the function of the crowd-sourced syllabus and how it interfaces with complex pedagogic parameters. Its role in navigating 'the event' was ignored in the push to leverage popularity and to interface education, literacy and learning within the capital interests of publication industries. The Trump1.0 syllabus closed down debate, rather than opening it up. It did not leverage the hashtag and its ambivalent, open-ended potential in providing a conduit for multiples to flow through and interact with 'the real'.

The crowd-sourced syllabus is part of the 'sharing economy' which deploys the unpaid labour of experts for 'the practices of sharing, exchange or rental of goods and services to others ... without the transfer of ownership'.[4] In this model, contributors to a project donate their time and expertise, for a variety of reasons including progress and altruism. Companies and organisations can cynically utilise crowd-sourcing as a 'virtual labour market'[5] that they do not have to compensate financially. In the neoliberal era, the free circulation of knowledge is a double-edged sword that often services those able to leverage knowledge as another form of rentier capitalism where the expertise of others is hijacked for the benefit of elites, while those in possession of that expertise are seduced to share so they can 'benefit' from this greed by monetising their materiality. Instead of the traditional abuses of 'land grabs'[6] enacted by rentiers to add more assets to their ownership portfolio, this is instead, an 'intellect grab'. The cogent caches of user-generated content and interactivity that social media networks monetise take the unpaid intellectual and cultural labour of people using the online space and profit. The idealising of this labour as a form of 'commons-based peer production'[7] that codifies a space of free circulation of ideas that no one person has ownership over neglects the tenacities of capitalism in colonising these spaces for profit. The crowd-sourced syllabus acknowledges but resists these tendencies to commodify and to idealise the nature of sharing, recognising that nuanced understandings of exchange mean that there is potency in what emerges in contemporary consciousness of the past as well as the present. The sharing of provocative pasts, radical thinking and cultures of educated hope mobilises 'asynchronous linkages'[8] that challenge the contemporary constructs of valid and valuable knowing.

When the sharing involves the circulation of ideas and information that resist easy capitalisation, neat insertion into neoliberal normalities and even reject the dominant narratives of knowledge use, new potentialities are enacted. Different memories are conjured and space for unstable ideas to emerge that have not yet been sedated and shaped by the dominant interests of a time is opened. Part of the atomisation of alternatives and denial of difference is the control over these forces of visualisation and representation – of what is possible and past. Crowd-sourcing can be dislodged from the digital economy as another form of wealth generation, and beyond its democratic ideals as open-sourced salvation from capitalism. It is a tool which provides a locus for contemporary evolutions of political economies of interaction that are yet to settle into dominant and subordinate positions or be colonised by specific forms of thinking and being. This is not as simple as asserting that the crowd displays an organic intelligence through leveraging diverse ways of knowing to develop radical insights and inspirational leaps in knowing that an individual cannot. It is subtle. Sources mobilised by the crowd create complexities of knowing, revelling in repressed truths, that both interface with and reject educational infrastructures and common sense. The crowd is unpredictable. It will harvest knowledges long forgotten, hidden and masked because they provide meaning within their everyday 'real' and service knowing that is unsanctioned and unofficial. The crowd will identify and fill gaps in unruly ways. The crowd-sourced syllabus undermines the competitive nature of knowing by reaching back into complexities and critical consciousness of the past to reject the stripping of knowledge from disempowered groups in the present. The emergence of the precariat as a central identity of the neoliberal era stimulates new forms of knowledge creation for the crowd-sourced syllabus. 'The precariat has a weakened sense of "social memory"'[9] and the crowd-sourced syllabus lengthens it enabling a politicisation of the precariat as a point of contention in the present to awaken the repressed truth of reproletarianisation currently being enacted.

The Trump1.0 syllabus undermined the organic and contestable nature of the crowd-sourced syllabus not because it was created by educators and scholars but because it was deployed by empowered interests in publishing to leverage its popularity in an intellect grab for *The Chronicle Review*. This blunder led to the creation of the Trump2.0 syllabus curated by N.D.B. Connolly and Keisha N. Blain which significantly expanded and complicated the reading list by subject and material. The Trump3.0 Syllabus emerged in January 2017. It was compiled by Nyron Crawford, an Assistant Professor of Political Science and Matt Wray, Associate Professor of Sociology, both at Temple University in Philadelphia. This syllabus was published at *Public Books*, an online magazine devoted to engaging a 'model for connecting scholarship and public life'[10] that re-deployed the role of the public intellectual and re-energised the potential of the crowd-sourced syllabus.

As a nexus between civic debate and anti-intellectual culture, the syllabus was aimed at being an antidote to the narrowing of public consciousness. Publishing it at *Public Books* was an attempt to combat what Henry Giroux has called 'civic illiteracy'[11] and as a buffer against the 'intellectual violence'[12] inflicted by Trump during his election campaign in vocalising sexist, racist and ableist rhetoric. The suspicion levelled at experts is cajoled and resisted by *Public Books* which affirms radical thinking and critical debate in response to declining public conversation. As neoliberalism arose in the postwar period, many on the Left absconded into identarian postmodernity, abandoning rigorous and meaningful intervention in capitalism. Many were 'left behind' by the supposed global riches of free markets which were subsidised by the cheap labour markets of the third world. They were further displaced when migration was celebrated by the Left as an exemplar of social tolerance and equity, inviting those cheap markets into the 'first world', permanently undermining any chance of the working poor and the precariat to advocate, resist or rebel against these conditions. Strategies for understanding these processes were few and far between. The educated elite was the target for their smug comfort in ignoring the insidiousness of capitalism, espousing 'global village' naiveté and championing identity politics and social justice while the very structures that were installed to support and sustain social equity were being undermined and dismantled. These gentrified debates about difference, diversity, globalisation, human rights and economics did little to mollify the discarded classes who were faced with realities of survival and fewer tools to navigate these conditions. Education appeared to increasingly obscure and abstract 'the real'. It no longer offered people tools to make sense of the everyday. Instead it made the everyday dissociate from the ordinary. When the banks were bailed out of the 2008 financial crisis with public money unavailable to ordinary people, the rhetoric of the market economy was explicitly and overtly contradicted. Government intervention was acceptable to prop up the neoliberal machinery when it suited. That money was not available to individuals, undermining the overwhelming ideologies that asserted that households and governments were equal. The elite languages used to explain these processes were evidence of the collusion of education with the moneyed class – and the allying of education with employment and social mobility in neoliberalism undermined any alternative knowledges that might critique these assumptions.

Trump's success has been frequently connected to the triumphant rhetoric of fascism in cultivating division, narrowing debate and marginalising others. His presidency mobilises a new fascism arriving out of anger and resentment. He affirms a simplistic vision of the world where clear-cut, uncomplicated answers will resolve all the problems, rejecting the nuances offered through higher education and solidifying (a universal) 'common sense'. It is seductive. When people are alienated from work and education and when public debate swings between being too complex and excessively jingoistic, the clarity of the strong-(wo)man is enticing to those who have been bamboozled by double-speak and sold lies about the state of their lives and their capacity to live meaningfully within it. Importantly, they are told that the reason their lives remain difficult is because there has been too much meddling from intellectual elites in the state of the world and the way to liberation is to reject all reasonable critical thought and embrace the emotional truths that are located in the (irrational) proximity of their experiences. In the rejection of intellectualism they are free to fill up their stories with any truths they see fit. This is how Trump's contrary and confounding rhetoric is appealing. You can map your experience on top of it with little difficulty. Even his overt and obvious flouting of the logics of debate and truth-telling is somehow endearing as it speaks to the ego inside us all wanting to be the champion of our own worlds. His human frailty presented as sheer hubris, arrogance and audacity to embody all that is often critiqued about politics – the value of appearance over action, the malleability of meanings in the service of power and authority, the simpering placating and gerrymandering of support – in this there is an odd level of honesty in Trump's insidious performance of ego-authority that offers comfort in a faulty seeing-what-you-get that voters hail as a truth-performance. It is this pseudo-honesty-in-deception that connects him to fascism with multiple commentators directly correlating Trump with Hitler – though this is mostly connected to Trump's fondness for rallies where an adoring crowd cheers him. Others have correlated him with Mussolini.[13]

Fascism flourishes in contemporary times because its antidote is critical thinking. To think critically today with the scale of information available on the internet and the paucity of functional and critical literacies to interpret these ways of knowing, as well as when and how information intersects with the offline world, coupled with the neutering of education and public intellectual culture, is fatiguing. This absence has led to the flourishing of the right wing where easy 'common sense' languages and understandings fill the gaps of public debate. It is a refusal to complexity – a misreading of the refusal to be dominated, by inviting a different form of domination into engagement with the self and society. In the space of the hashtag, this refusal is conjured and rewritten. The ambiguities of refusing are revisioned, by activating an archive of resources, connected and contrasted – a heterotopia of knowing that mobilises space for the radical and repressed to emerge. In order to make sense of Donald Trump and his election, the hashtag is put to use, opening a space for the cries and crises of his support base to be shaped and defined alongside and through the critical real and the knowledges of dispossession. Importantly, the Trump syllabi do not originate nor do they rigorously deploy the hashtag. The syllabus that is conjured and connected to the Trump syllabi is the New Fascism Syllabus which has leveraged the hashtag to open up greater complexities to the networks of knowledge that are needed to interrupt the contemporary common sense.

Immediately after the election of Donald Trump in November 2016 Dr Elizabeth Heinman, a professor of German History at the University of

Iowa, launched the hashtag #NewFascismSyllabus. Unlike the Trump syllabi, which in its versions relied on academic authors, #NewFascismSyllabus is a cohesively crowd-sourced project launched on social media. Its Facebook page solicits contributions and the Facebook group brings together scholars to discuss and debate the emergence of neo-fascist movements.

> *History is being made in real time.*
>
> *Drawing inspiration from the important work of those who pulled together the Charleston Syllabus in the wake of the violence in SC, Jennifer Evans (Carleton) and Lisa Heineman (Iowa) are soliciting articles, relevant news stories, analyses, Op/Eds, historical essays – anything to help contextualize the current state of play. The focus need not solely be on Trump's Presidency. The rise of the neo-right goes beyond borders.*
>
> *You can find us @NewFascSyllabus on Twitter. Post, message, re-tweet, just be sure to add #newfascsyllabus and #twitterstorians to your post.*[14]

The syllabus is divided into two broad sections: Interrogating the Past and Interrogating the Present. In Interrogating the Past, the first item in the syllabus proper is Walter Benjamin's, 'Theories of German Fascism: On the collection of essays *War and Warrior*, edited by Ernst Jünger', which is a critique of sloppy critical thinking and writing. Benjamin accuses the writers of an 'unrefined, thoroughly journalistic haste to capitalise on the present without grasping the past'.[15] It is an indictment on fascist thinking and rhetoric, pointing to the ways in which ignorance is perpetuated through clever manipulation of the past via emotive calls to nationalism. However, to start with this reading asks a lot of the reader. For the layperson who has no previous knowledge of Benjamin or the context in which he is writing, this article is impenetrable and confusing. In order for this reading to make sense, the reader must have a high level of independent motivation as well as literacy skills in information management. Benjamin's argument is framed by his status, as a German Jew. He was objecting to the manipulation of memories being leveraged to validate closed-mindedness and a reckless disregard for life woven into a toxic nationalism. The reader must be able to make the connections between the post-World-War-I context of German society and the emergent experiences of the twenty-first century, as well as the role of language in constructing and crafting the realities and truths of a time and place. In presenting this article at the start of the syllabus #NewFascismSyllabus adopts an andragogic approach to teaching and learning. Even though the syllabus is structured in a didactic manner with material divided into cogent weekly topics to direct the trajectory through the subject matter, the reading list itself assumes a relatively high level of comprehension regarding fascism, and an ability to deploy information literacy to build learning structures for the self.

Andragogy is a magical term that both acknowledges that adults learn differently from children but masks the ways in which adult learners require learning literacies in the same way that children do – that is, they also need to learn how to learn. To that end, andragogy exists in tension with the standardised modes of learning and concepts of literacy that punctuate conventional educational research. Andragogy is most often deployed using the functional framework mapped out by Knowles that situates six traits of adult learners as they are differentiated from children.[16] This structure gives a solid grounding on which to build an understanding of how adults deploy information into knowledge differently from children. This is important in considering how university education is defined and enacted in curriculum design and in classroom teaching practices. However, critics of Knowles argue that his model considers 'the learning process and the individual to be separated from the social, political, economic and historical context'[17] and so disregards a core feature of how knowledge is activated and deployed as well as how adults create complex interfaces with learning. Most notably, it does not account for the what has been called 'lifewide' learning 'which comprised not only institutionalised forms of learning but also self-directed, partly purposeful, and non-purposeful forms of learning'.[18] Idealised assertions about andragogy as a form of life-long learning involves assumptions about adult motivation, self-direction and resilience in developing new ideas and knowledges and fails to acknowledge that adults are not always 'competent by virtue of their own experiences'[19] and that they indeed may not be cogently self-directive. Instead, learning can sometimes be piecemeal, spontaneous and anarchic, deployed with haphazard literacies and half-formed ideas. Learning may erupt out of circumstances driven by a collision of external and internal factors. Whilst curiosity, anxiety about the present and the future or expansion of an already existing knowledge-base may have brought adults to the #NewFascismSyllabus, apart from a few framing questions at the start of each module, there is little guidance on what to do with or how to interpret the material. This assumes naturalness with the knowledges one would encounter in a conventional schooling circumstance, deploying a familiar range of cues and codes to people exposed to a formalised learning environment. The #NewFascismSyllabus then is not a radical departure offering up a revolutionary rethink of teaching and learning in a digital environment. Nor is it a potent intervention in the rise of neo-fascist rhetoric and governance.

It deploys an agenda of a critical interrogation of the real from a position of high-order literacy in scholarship and learning.

The reading material is an intervention into alt-right political trajectories emerging globally and a perceived lack of debate and critical thinking about the behaviours and attitudes of right-wing leaders and pundits. Instead, an easy slip into cheerleading and the seduction of strong (wo)man rhetoric is currently being advanced. Journalists are not intervening in their role as the fourth estate and are instead in service of media barons whose business of selling news has manoeuvred into the selling of scandal. Major television networks even offer the alt-right air-time in the interests of so-called unbiased reporting. Consider an example from Australia where mainstream network Channel Seven's morning news and current affairs program 'Sunrise' has regularly paid Pauline Hanson, the leader of right-wing political party One Nation, to appear on their programme. She has been part of commentary on vaccinations, the housing crisis, private health cover, literacy and numeracy, flag burning and any number of other topics that she has not demonstrated any expertise in.[20] Her appearances have been justified by executive producer Michael Pell as offering viewers 'both sides of the story'.[21] This is a familiar refrain by television executives who are masking their push for ratings by binarising divisive and oppositional individuals in discussions on 'hot topics'. This is not an effort for balanced reporting, but an intent to stir controversy by reifying opinion as considered thinking. The #NewFascismSyllabus is an antidote to this surface engagement by offering up 'deep-thinking' as a pathway to reflexive analysis of emerging trends in global debate. Its assumption of the intelligence of the reader is part of this antidote – assuming levels of literacy in enacting an educated hope. This is a refusal of ignorance. It appears to reassert old ideals about elite education to the exclusion of those who have not had access to these literacies. However, its demand that readers make connections to their own previous knowledge within the ambiguities of a digitised, dislodged and disintermediated interface is where the work of learning occurs. The syllabus is disconnected from any formal learning outcomes. It is a pick and mix learning framework. While the syllabus has a linear structure there is no prescription to a learner's interaction with it. It does not preclude jumping from module to module. Learning is an intimate process of individuals making their own way through the material and interacting with it, and of not having to account for their interpretations to classmates or a more knowledgeable teacher. This does not mean learners are free to make their own assumptions. Nor does it mean no challenging or destabilising of their internal worlds of thought and assumption. The syllabus is a dialogue between the past and the present, drawing clear parallels and asking readers to do connective work to provoke and persist. The everyday 'real' invokes repressed truths that are difficult to visualise and understand. The syllabus stands in contrast to the easy answers offered by neo-fascists.

The 13 weeks of Interrogating the Past in the #NewFascismSyllabus are populated with academic texts from Umberto Eco, through to Paul Gilroy and Amrita Basu. It also suggests primary documents and cultural works including the films *Downfall* and *Pan's Labyrinth* as well as an examination of Picasso's painting *Guernica* and George Orwell's *Homage to Catalonia*. It models the diversity of literacies that now constitute effective learning strategies and complicates a network of knowledges that contribute to how sense is made of the everyday through both high and low culture. The higher-order thinking conjured by the syllabus is *the* intervention into fascism as a rejection of simple and seductive thinking. It does not take too much thinking to see through Trump and his ilk. The rise of fascism relies on a wilful ignorance that #NewFascismSyllabus rejects. It is the combination of resources offered by the syllabus that reifies the actions and mental reflexivity required to access complex modes of thinking and knowing. By moving from Walter Benjamin to *Pan's Labyrinth*, space for critical interrogation as well as reflection is modelled in the materials selected for the syllabus.

The evental context for the creation of the New Fascism Syllabus is pregnant with perceptions and politics. The hashtag emphasis on 'new' offers the radical intervention in asserting that fascism is not located in the long past and archaic ideas of national potency and racial superiority deployed by the Axis powers of World War II. The #NewFascismSyllabus brings it into the present and situates struggles for knowledge within the arrival of the alt-right, global populism and a merging of the past with the present. Radical thinking emerges within a framework of educated hope where knowledge of the past is presented as key to understanding and tracking how these ideas move into the present. It is a precursor to activism, providing the tools to refuse not just fascism, but ignorance and easy pathways to knowing.

The #NewFascismSyllabus is a fusing of approaches that is formed in the values of Enlightenment connected to the development of the individual and also the progress of society – importantly, however, it is also aimed at working through the social and political contexts of hatred by deploying rigour and complexity to counteract lazy thinking and simple solutions to the everyday difficulties people face in their understanding of their life circumstances. In the second part of the syllabus entitled: Interrogating the Present, a less formalised structure is presented enabling learners to meander their way through the material. It is a gathering of essays and opinion pieces that interact with these ideas as they have arisen in context. This part of the syllabus is open and less prescriptive. Most are pieces of journalism and only 5 of the 89 resources date before 2013. This is a map of commentary that circulates and is emergent out of the contemporary alt-right conditions predominantly in the United States but contextualised globally. A core debate about the extent and type of fascism embodied by Trump is the central theme of this material divided into eight subject areas: Fascism, Authoritarianism, Populism, Crisis of Neoliberalism/ Liberal Democracy, Cultural Studies Frameworks, Civil Society: Coordination and Resistance, Related Movements Outside of the United States, and Additional Resources. The material located within and about the present is organised to demonstrate the connections between ideas and articulate an extended archive of resources. The purpose is to model the range and type of information that can be gathered, read and understood – how repressed truths are hidden and can be conjured into learning pathways. Considered journalism, detailed polemics and critical theory are aligned, enabling learners to move through a variety of levels of critique. The seriousness of the fascist 'event' is asserted. Educated hope is the way forward. Double refusal is essential. A networked knowledge scaffold supports movement through these ideas. Detailed contextualisation demonstrates the nuances of how ideas circulate and the impact of politics, economics, language and power on social outcomes and the everyday real.

The #NewFascismSyllabus is a toolbox for refusal, providing a pathway from the past and into the present by offering up resources that have interrogated fascism and then demonstrating how these ideas are being deployed, engaged with and resisted in the present. The calibre of the syllabus and its structure suggests an archaic and formalised approach to learning that is prescriptive and even exclusionary; however, the composition of materials and the sectioning belie this approach. Instead of affirming an elite approach to knowledge – and even though much of the reading is scholarly and assuming an already literate learner – an intervention into fascism is being applied by the deployment of deep-thinking and 'lifewide' learning and an interrogation of the everyday 'real'. Life-long learning tropes that assert the importance of resilience in the face of such difficulties and an inability to change or intervene in them is displaced. Life-long learning operationalises the currencies of education and inserts it in the capitalist neoliberal economy of exchange. In *lifewide* learning, the person engages with the ideas that assist them in making sense of their current life situation and evolving consciousness of these conditions in relation to personal and political, local and global circumstance. The #NewFascismSyllabus connects the individual to the social and political contexts of time and space by mobilising the pasts through the digital disintermediated present. The hashtag permits this fluidity by providing a nexus at which contemporary disobedience with knowledge is conveyed, one that is simultaneously unapologetically rigorous and scholarly but also filled with commentary, reflexivity and critical engagement with the everyday. The syllabus is linear and formalised, but also open and mobile. It presents academic scholarly material alongside journalism, art and films. It assumes a level of literacy that can be construed as exclusionary, but deploys this as an important intervention into the ignorance and alienation cultivated by fascism in asserting the assumed intelligence of learners, including them in knowledge creation and asking them to engage in 'deep-thinking' which can lead to critical thinking – the ultimate antidote to fascism.

NOTES

1. N.D.B. Connolly, Keisha N. Blain, Chad Williams, Stephen G. Hall, and Leah Wright, "Trump Syllabus is as White as the Man Himself," *The Chronicle of Higher Education*, June 23, 2016, https://www.chronicle.com/article/Trump-Syllabus-Is-as/236899.
2. The Chronicle Review, "Trump 101," June 19, 2016, https://www.chronicle.com/article/Trump-Syllabus/236824.
3. Connolly, Blain, Williams, Hall, and Wright, "Trump Syllabus is as White as the Man Himself,"
4. Araz Taeihagh, "Crowdsourcing, Sharing Economies and Development," *Journal of Developing Societies* 33, no. 2, (2017): 192, https://doi.org/10.1177/0169796X17710072.
5. Araz Taeihagh, "Crowdsourcing, sharing economies and development," *Journal of Developing Societies*, 33, no. 2, (2017): 191–222, https://doi.org/10.1177/0169796X17710072
6. David Harvey, *Seventeen Contradictions and the End of Capitalism* (Oxford: Oxford University Press, 2014), 77.
7. Robbie T. Nakatsu, Elissa B. Grossman, and Charalambos L. Iacovou, "A Taxonomy of Crowdsourcing Based on task complexity," *Journal of Information Science* 40, no. 6, (2014): 825, https://doi.org/10.1177/0165551514550140.
8. Nakatsu, Grossman, and Iacovou, "A Taxonomy of Crowdsourcing," 829.
9. Guy Standing, *The Precariat: The New Dangerous Class* (London: Bloomsbury, 2011), 23.
10. Henry A. Giroux, "Public Intellectuals Today," *Arena Magazine*, no. 128, (Feb/Mar 2014): 42.
11. Giroux, "Public Intellectuals Today," 44.
12. Giroux, "Public Intellectuals Today," 45.
13. Fedja Buric, "Trump's not Hitler, He's Mussolini: How GOP Anti-intellectualism Create a Modern Fascist Movement in America," *Salon*, March 12, 2016, https://www.salon.com/2016/03/11/trumps_not_hitler_hes_mussolini_how_gop_anti_intellectualism_created_a_modern_fascist_movement_in_america/.

14. New Fascism Syllabus, About Page, *Facebook*, accessed January 27, 2020, https://www.facebook.com/pg/NewFascismSyllabus/about/?ref=page_internal.
15. Walter Benjamin, "Theories of German Fascism: On the Collection of Essays War and Warrior, edited by Ernst Jünger," *New German Critique* 17, (1979): 122, http://www.jstor.org/stable/488013.
16. Malcolm Knowles, *The Modern Practice of Adult Education: From Pedagogy to Andragogy* (Cambridge: Prentice Hall, 1980).
17. Svein Loeng, "Various Ways of Understanding the Concept of Andragogy," *Cogent Education* 5, no. 1, (2018): 5, https://doi.org/10.1080/2331186X.2018.1496643.
18. Loeng, "Various Ways of Understanding the Concept of Andragogy," 7.
19. Loeng, "Various Ways of Understanding the Concept of Andragogy," 8.
20. Importantly, there are other commentators she is paired with who also are not experts in these subjects.
21. Robb Stott, "It's Too Late Now: The Time for Sunrise to Reject Pauline Hanson was Years Ago," *Junkee*, March 18, 2019, https://junkee.com/pauline-hanson-sunrise/198085.

6

#STANDINGROCKSYLLABUS

Actual resistance demands an understanding of history through relations of power.[1]

#NoDAPL began its life as a hashtag in 2016 as part of an ongoing resistance enacted by Indigenous water protectors against settler extractive industries infrastructure. The Dakota Access Pipeline (DAPL) runs from the Bakken oil fields in Northwest Dakota through South Dakota and ends in Illinois. It was diverted from its original route just north of the predominantly white city of Bismarck close to within half a mile of the Standing Rock Sioux (Oceti Sakowin) Reservation border where along its route it threatened not only sacred sites but also the integrity of the water supply. It had been moved from its original route near Bismarck due to concern over 'proximity to wellhead source water protection areas'.[2] The pipeline's new route crossing the Missouri River and tunnelling under Lake Oahe threatens sacred sites and presents a potential environmental challenge to the water supply for the Standing Rock Reservation and the Cheyenne River Reservation. The area and its tribes have already been subjected to a long history of environmental violence and water theft. The intersecting Cannonball River within Oceti Sakowin territory, also under threat from pipeline spills, had been diverted from its original flow to make way for the Oahe Dam in the 1960s. The water protector movement that arose in 2016 was predominantly young people who had grown up in knowledge of this exploitation. The ReZpect Our Water movement which kick-started the Standing Rock protests was led by young members of the tribe. Tokata Iron Eyes and Anna Lee Rain Yellowhammer are two of the young people who led the social media campaign to draw attention to the violations of the DAPL. They launched crowd-funding campaigns, recorded YouTube videos and posted on social media to spotlight resistance and recruit allies. They deployed the slogan 'Mni Wiconi' meaning 'water is life' to situate their centrality in environmental and sustainability issues connected to a decolonisation of the knowledges that determine how ecologies are managed and maintained.

In April 2017, Standing Rock Oceti Sakowin Tribe Elder LaDonna Brave Bull Allard established the first camp at the Standing Rock Reservation to provide a 'prayer camp' mobilising the sacred site of ceremony and ancestral knowledge that they were fighting to preserve in protecting the water.

> *In her telling, Allard emphasizes that the true name for the Cannonball River is Inyan Wakangapi Wakpa, which means 'River That Makes the Sacred Stones'. This name refers to a once active whirlpool whose movement shaped 'large, spherical sandstone formations' in the river's bed. Back in the 1950s, however, the U.S. Corps of Engineers severed this flow when they flooded the area for the construction of the Oahe Dam. The project resulted in a loss of 150,000 acres for the Cheyenne River Indian Reservation. But the greater loss was not quantifiable or limited to one Nation or another. Allard writes, 'They killed a portion of our sacred river. I was a young girl when the floods came and desecrated our burial sites and Sundance grounds. Our people are in that water. This river holds the story of my entire life'.*[3]

The DAPL is a $US3.8 billion construction that has largely bypassed environmental impact assessment, which is how it gained permission to pass through and in close proximity to Indigenous lands. It is suggested that the pipeline has been

> *...fast-tracked from the beginning, using the Nationwide Permit 12 process that treats the pipeline as a series of small construction sites and grants exemption from the environmental review required by the Clean Water Act and the National Environmental Policy Act.*[4]

This is an example of how Indigenous land rights are routinely and randomly bypassed by bureaucratic railroading strategies of 'Decide, Announce, Defend'[5] designed to entrench and justify decisions rather than engage in meaningful public participation. Such approaches are consistent with history. As of the late twentieth century, 'America has yet to keep one Indian treaty or agreement despite the fact the United States government signed over four hundred such treaties and agreements with Indian tribes'.[6] The oldest of these treaties dates back to 1794.[7] Indigenous communities are increasingly resisting this dismissal as they themselves deploy the legal machinery to generate protections against such violations. Naomi Klein has shown how Indigenous communities in Canada are providing the last line of defence against environmental abuse and callous exploitation of the land for profit.

> ...in many cases, the movements against extreme energy extraction are becoming more than just battles against specific oil, gas, and coal companies and more, even, than pro-democracy movements. They are opening up spaces for a historical reconciliation between Indigenous peoples and non-Natives, who are finally understanding that, at a time when elected officials have open disdain for basic democratic principles, Indigenous rights are not a threat, but a tremendous gift. Because the original Indigenous treaty negotiators in much of North America had the foresight to include language protecting their right to continue living off their traditional lands, they bequeathed to all residents of these and many other countries the legal tools to demand that our governments refrain from finishing the job of flaying the planet.[8]

Klein maps legal interpretations of invasion era treaties asserting that in retaining the right to 'hunt, fish, and trap on their territory'[9] Indigenous communities did not cede their land but instead shared it, and governments or corporations acting on the land cannot infringe upon Indigenous communities' continued rights to use it. Indigenous treaties, while having been largely ignored throughout the history of colonisation,[10] are now serving as the ballast for the environmental movement.

This is not a repetition of colonial exploitation where settlers conveniently find themselves utilising Indigenous resilience and defiance when their lifestyles are threatened by pollution. Indigenous peoples provide the raw material and the model for the double refusal via a culture of endurance. While litigation dominates and the rule of law is being deployed by capitalists to bend natural and cultural resources to their will, their reliance on tricky legalese is doubling back as law courts are upholding Indigenous land and water rights as well as native title, particularly since the United Nations Declaration on the Rights of Indigenous Peoples in 2007. By activating endurance, Indigenous peoples bypass the contemporary politics of resilience which promotes a stoic resignation to the exploitations being faced in deploying the tools to cope with rather than transform these conditions. Instead, Indigenous peoples draw on a reconfiguration of time that bypasses enlightened modernity, reaching back into temporalities that confound the forward momentum of linear progress and development and instead embrace aeons of fluctuations within ecosystems and humanity's relationship to the earth. For Indigenous peoples 'resilience is one part of endurance, the other dimension being time'.[11] This reification of time ignores the assertions of modernity that progress is linear and instead affirms the cyclical longevity of being. Endurance becomes a dominant trope for Indigenous meaning systems whereby the tools and tenacities to exist in the face of genocide and ongoing annihilation of language, beliefs, peoples, land and cultures is more than resilient. It is the transformation of suffering into defiance by holding onto communal and cultural truths across transcendental temporalities. This is a test of character over generations.

At Standing Rock, the Indigenous community came together in an unprecedented demonstration of solidarity with over 90 tribes represented at one of the biggest 'gatherings since Little Bighorn in 1877'.[12] A Council Lodge – 'a special tepee that functioned as a gathering site for Sioux leaders [which] had not been erected since the nineteenth century' – was established to gather the leadership together in solidarity and cohesion. A variety of social media sites and hashtags punctuated the movement including #nodapl, #standingrock, #waterislife and #rezpectourwater that mobilised Indigenous and non-Native allies in support of the protest.[13] Online it was reported that 'at least 1.3 million Facebook users checked in virtually at Oceti Sakowin and other Indigenous camps and communities to ensure that support presence was recognised'.[14] When the stand-off between the protestors, police[15] and private security[16] hired by Energy Transfer Partners became violent and the water protectors were attacked with tear gas, rubber bullets, water cannons and acoustic weaponry, over 2,000 military veterans arrived to help protect protesters and form a human shield.[17] Standing Rock has stimulated an outpouring of collectivity, solidarity and communication between allies, Indigenous and non-Native protesters, water protectors, environmental activists, academics, scholars and journalists. 'Standing for' and 'Standing with' Standing Rock have become crucial catchphrases conjuring consolidation with the protestors by allies who cannot or for political, economic, historical, or social reasons, do not wish to occupy the physical protest space at Standing Rock. Their defiance takes shape not only on the ground but also in online spaces, through films, in song, poetry, photography, journalism and scholarship that articulate narratives counter to the stories being told about Indigenous peoples, water protectors and protesters by police and other authorities – namely that they are unlawful, aggressive and violent.

#NoDAPL is a declaration of defiance. The overt refusal of the hashtag is the opening act of a potential double refusal. It is a refusal to be dominated. #NoDAPL is a rejection of power and of the assertion and insertion of corporate governance on Indigenous land. Importantly, in this initial refusal, it opens space for a refusal to dominate to unfurl. This is embraced by the

#StandingRockSyllabus, an ally to the #NoDAPL refusal in offering a curated and prolific cross-disciplinary archive of documents, readings, maps and artefacts that present a context in which the protests have emerged, situated within and in response to, over 500 years of exploitation, dispossession and demonisation by governing authorities and the institutions supported and maintained by colonial thought.

The syllabus was created by The New York City Stands with Standing Rock Collective, a group of 15 activists and scholars who single out doctoral student Matthew Chrisler as kick-starting the syllabus by mapping 'a timeline of events that contextualises DAPL within treaty history in the Plains, but specifically Sioux treaty history'.[18] This Collective generated the syllabus in solidarity with the protestors at Standing Rock with the aim of providing a backdrop for the protests and an expanding reference for the historical factors that intersect through land, race, authority, resistance, the environment, governance, sustainability and violence at the site.

> ...we are interested in supporting and contextualizing the Standing Rock struggle within literatures that can help those new to Sioux history and contemporary Indigenous politics and criticism to understand this issue within history, within the literature on toxicity and its dangers to the environment, and within gender and police violence within settler states.[19]

The syllabus is rigorous and subject to stringent review for its scholarly significance as well its diversity governed by the importance of representing cohesive pasts, provocative presents and speculative futures. The authors placed emphasis on the curatorial nature of the online syllabus and how the materials would work as a whole, its relevance to protestors on the ground in Standing Rock as well as other students and scholars and people interested in the subject area. To this end, 'identifying scholarship by Sioux scholars, other Indigenous scholars, and allied settler scholars became a deliberative curatorial exercise in radical accountability to Indigenous thought and politics'.[20] To achieve a comprehensive syllabus that was rooted in Indigenous knowledges and scholarship, including an overarching trajectory of endurance and educated hope, required the pooling of Indigenous scholars and the acknowledgement of materials outside of the range of the compiling authors. They acknowledge there were 'certain materials that we wanted to include but felt inadequate to interpret. So we direct educators and students to the crucial archives of Lakota Winter Counts'[21] a pictorial history of tribal events that predates publishing.

The syllabus can be taught in its entirety or divided up into smaller portions for people to delve into as their interest takes them.[22] It is aimed at all levels of learning from schools to university, at protests and in legal preparations. Similarly, the topics covered range from autobiographical works to maps, journalism, photographs and scholarly material. It is divided into 15 sections. Importantly, the works included in the syllabus have been removed from behind paywalls, and this objective, to free up knowledge, is stated as one of the crucial aims of the #StandingRockSyllabus. The Standing Rock YouTube channel provides a series of videos filmed at the University of Columbia in October 2016 at a 'teach-in' – a form of teaching as resistance where knowledge is deployed in the service of disobedience and alternative ways of knowing and being. In the age of neoliberal education, these are critical pedagogies that educate for social change instead of employability. They are built upon 'sit-ins' where protestors peacefully occupy physical space, usually reserved for authority, to protest and quietly resist.[23] Teach-ins have their origins in the protests against the Vietnam War. The objective is to inform and be informed about events and the contexts which motivate the emergence of specific actions and authoritarian activities. Teach-ins have been used by the Occupy Wall Street movement as well as Black Lives Matter. They convey the importance of education to social change and reify the centrality of learning and knowing to resistance movements. Radical education creates solidarity by reifying communal connections and validating indigenous ways of knowing along horizontal links rather than hierarchies of power and the linearities of formal education. Alternatives are created and visualised, enacted and embraced. The narratives of the past are presented in school curricula mobilising critical pedagogies in the present, generating significant consequences for how 'memory and justice are intricately linked'.[24] Importantly, for Standing Rock and other Indigenous movements is the significance of shifting knowledge to place-based ways of knowing rather than the linear temporalities favoured by European histories in modernity. Connecting the land to a transcendent past challenges these established knowledge constructs and the sense-making scaffolds of temporality. The management of time and knowledge mediated through history and modernity curtails the crisis of the 'over-abundance of books and the frailty of human resources for mastering them (such as memory and time)'.[25] Indigenous knowledges passed through aeons via storytelling, cultural practices and ritual operates in tension with contemporary calls for justice and accountability as 'attention to temporal continuities' and linear renderings of cause and effect are a crucial settler strategy to mapping historical wrongs and their impact on present-day tribes.[26] The incompatibilities of temporal understandings are a source of conflict. The assertions of linear continuity of time through which the unity of the self and its connections to geographic cohesion are measured offer an inherently

European frame through which to view and render experiences of the past. The reliance on contained temporalities and linearity overrides the dispersed and flattened understandings of space, region and ancient ancestry that punctuate Indigenous knowledges. The rationalities upon which truth claims are asserted and reified work within the temporalities of enlightened modernity and its onward march towards progress and human development increasingly defined by extractive technologies and exploitative innovation. It is in this context that 'the world as lived through these days feels more like a contraption for forgetting rather than a setting for learning'.[27] Indigenous memories are denied and settler memories are solidified, but 'such a solidly entrenched memory seems potentially incapacitating in many cases, misleading in many more, useless in most'.[28] Indigenous knowledges challenge the hierarchies of temporality as understood in conventional and convenient historical knowledge. The dispersal and flattened realities of transcendent temporality emboldened by Indigenous histories serve to deprioritise the enlightened self as a singular, coherent, unitary, secure and discrete mode of being. It is Indigenous approaches to knowledge and understanding the complex maps of spatio-temporal truths that can offer the multilayered literacies needed to navigate the contemporary explosions of dispersed, fragmented, interlinked and interdisciplinary knowledge. It is in these times and spaces that alternate knowledges circulate. The crowd-sourced syllabus is digitally mediating these relationships and opening new spaces for thinking through 'the event'.

#StandingRockSyllabus begins spatially with a series of maps illustrating the changing shape of Octei Sakowin Oyate territory and how various treaty negotiations and violations have changed the spatiality of the nation. These maps are framed as treaty boundaries rather than definitive borders of Octei Sakowin Oyate territory demonstrating how colonial definitions of land and identity have sought to limit and frame Oceti Sakowin people. It is spatialised, but nevertheless linear and bounded, seeking to locate the Octei Sakowin in place, defining them by European knowledge. Overlaid with these changing treaty boundaries is the terrain for resistance – the DAPL route – showing the original plan north of Bismarck and its new trajectory under Lake Oahe and its intimate proximity to the Standing Rock Reservation. This is then followed by a linear timeline of events from the 'discovery' of the United States in 1492 by Christopher Columbus. Columbus narrative is rewritten. The syllabus describes him as leading 'expeditions to the "New World"' involving 'the pursuit of gold, [whereby] Columbus and the colonists enslave and terrorise Indigenous inhabitants across the Antilles/Caribbean'.[29] The timeline does not champion European discovery, progress and civilisation, but is instead told from the perspective of Indigenous peoples who were part of these events but rarely presented as subjects whose experience was radically different to the dominant stories being told. Their evental truths are lost and locked up in their endurance strategies. This shifting perspective in the syllabus is in aid of presenting an accountability to the historical wrongs inflicted upon Indigenous peoples and how knowledges in the present continue to reify the experiences of racism and dispossession by refusing to account for different ways of being and knowing – on the land, in history and through the self. In this timeline, the American Revolution, for example, most often hailed as a moment of liberation of the United States from the British and a celebration of the foundation of the nation, is presented as a moment of disappointment for the disenfranchisement of Indigenous peoples and the 'enslavement of African-descendent peoples'.[30] Similarly, the Lewis and Clark Expedition of 1804, most radically rewritten into public consciousness in the twentieth century as opening up new passageways into the American West, is marked by their direct contact with the Oceti Sakowin whom they came into conflict and vilified upon their return. The timeline maps the significant events from the Indigenous perspective through the lens of settler history. It offers a contrasting and parallel narrative to the history most often presented of the United States connected to ideals of 'discovery' and American exceptionalism. The timeline narrows at 2014 to focus on the events at Standing Rock and the DAPL protest and it ends in 2016 at the apex of the stand-off and the creation of the syllabus.

The syllabus is then framed by a series of letters of support connecting the educational materials within the document to the ongoing resistance at the Standing Rock camp. Letters from the Faculty at Columbia University (where the first teach-in was held), the New School (where the second teach-in was held), Stony Brook University, The Center for Comparative Studies of Race and Ethnicity at Connecticut College and Binghamton University offer solidarity and support to the protestors. All express concern over the wilful disregard of Indigenous land and water rights by Energy Transfer Partners as well as the consistent violation of treaty rights and fears about the environmental damage oil spills might wreak on the populations who rely on the water supply of the Missouri and Cannonball Rivers, as well as Lake Oahe and the Ogallala Aquifer. These letters of support add scholarly verification to Standing Rock resistance and validate interpretations of history that resituate dominant narratives, reveal repressed truths and assert accountability for past wrongdoing.

The reading list is supplied in full with open access copies of the material photocopied, scanned or pasted directly into the document. The first reading centralises Indigenous voice and scholarship by presenting a conversation between J. Kēhaulani Kauanui and Patrick Wolfe about settler colonialism as a theory and practice. This article begins from the perspective of dissembling and troubling settler colonialism. Importantly, it reifies the use of 'settler' and not pilgrims or migrants to spotlight the structural language and meanings that seek to normalise invasion. This builds Wolfe's 2006 contention that 'settler colonisers come to stay: invasion is a structure not an event'.[31] This potent assertion calls to attention the ongoing *process* of colonisation and codifies its 'eventful' nature. It constantly reaffirms and reasserts itself, reclaiming the land over and over again. Indigenous peoples *endure* this remaking of settler colonialism and resist the codifications of Native-ness that accompany this fluidity. This is not resilience – a tactic to manage discomfort and displeasure. Endurance is an entrenched, defined and reified meaning system, in this case crafted over generations, that supports and sustains against long periods of trauma and exploitation.

> *these controversies also draw attention, in rather extreme ways, to the many, long temporalities at play in the settler colonial context – in this case temporalities that extend back nearly 10,000 years. The temporal dimensions of settler colonialism are multiple, syncopated, and move in many different directions. While settler colonialism and indigeneity endure, they do so in relation to many times.*[32]

Acknowledging the complexities and injustices of settler/Native reactivities and negotiations denies the civilising and progressive narratives of 'discovery' and triumph over an unruly landscape that has so often dominated narratives about white people in the rural lands of the United States. Importantly, it is also a conversation and centralises the telling of stories, orality, expression and engagement between perspectives as a dominant trope for troubling conventional ideals.

It is, therefore, significant that the Standing Rock syllabus concludes with images taken at the protector camp of the people, activists, landscapes and water. The photographs document solidarity. There are few pictures of the police and none of the violence that was to beset the camp. The images celebrate the protection of the land and the water, as a hopeful process. The narratives attached to the images tell of daily routines and communal life. They recode the time and space to open perspectives that represent ongoing endurance. They also illustrate the importance of digitised communication. The protestors meticulously recorded and documented their interactions with each other as well as security and police on Facebook, Twitter and Instagram. Video was streamed live as documentary footage of the unfolding events held police and protestors accountable to the words, actions and ideologies they embodied. The #StandingRockSyllabus provides the space for these enduring refusals and tenuously reveals the infrastructures of dispossession that may lead to the potential evental moment of Standing Rock. #StandingRockSyllabus activates theoretical intersections of the hashtag and its fluidities, enabling a syllabus to be built and an archive of knowledge to be conjured facilitating the opening of the double refusal. This double refusal takes place within an acknowledgement of endurance – the survival of Indigenous peoples. The syllabus is not aimed at pitting the Native against the settler – refusing the domination of the settler only to assert other forms of domination. By recognising the mobility of settler colonialism and endurance of Indigenous peoples, the emphasis is on how power, the land, the water and life are shared and how reconciliation is enacted and meaningful. Standing Rock *becomes* evental through the facility of the hashtag and the multiples that swirl within the void composed around and through the repressed truths of settler colonisation. Through sheer persistence, survival and endurance, Indigenous peoples peel open the spaces closed off by colonial rhetoric never allowing it to stand and instead inserting their own Standing Rock refusal, asserting the work of educated hope.

NOTES

1. Sandy Grande, Natalie Avalos, Jason Mancini, Christopher Newell, and endawnis Spears, "Red Praxis: Lessons from Mashantucket to Standing Rock," in *Standing with Standing Rock: Voices from the #NODAPL Movement*, eds. Nick Estes and Jaskrian Dhillon (Minneapolis: University of Minnesota Press, 2019), 256.
2. Amy Dalrymple, "Pipeline Route Plan First Called for Crossing North of Bismarck," *Bismarck Tribune*, August 18, 2016, https://bismarcktribune.com/news/state-and-regional/pipeline-route-plan-first-called-for-crossing-north-of-bismarck/article_64d053e4-8a1a-5198-a1dd-498d386c933c.html.
3. Tomoki Mari Birkett and Teresa Montoya, "For Standing Rock: A Moving Dialogue," in *Standing with Standing Rock: Voices from the #NODAPL Movement*, eds. Nick Estes and Jaskrian Dhillon (Minneapolis: University of Minnesota Press, 2019), 270.
4. Gail Ablow, "What You Need to Know about the Dakota Access Pipeline Protest," *Common Dreams*, September 9, 2016, https://www.commondreams.org/views/2016/09/09/what-you-need-know-about-dakota-access-pipeline-protest.
5. Taylor N. Johnson, "The Dakota Access Pipeline and the Breakdown of Participatory Processes in Environmental Decision-making," *Environmental Communication* 13, no. 3, (2019): 339.
6. Vine Deloria Jr, *Custer Died for Your Sins: An Indian Manifesto* (Normal: University of Oklahoma Press, 1988), 28.
7. The Pickering Treaty signed between the United States and the Seneca Tribe of the Iriquois Nation.

8. Naomi Klein, *This Changes Everything* (London: Penguin Books, 2014), 380.
9. Klein, *This Changes Everything*, 378.
10. Mary Louise Cappelli argues "Of the more than 500 negotiated treaties negotiated by the U.S. Federal Government with Native American Indian Tribes, 500 of these were also broken," Mary Louise Cappelli, "Standing with Standing Rock: Affective Alignment and Artful Resistance at the Native Nations Rise March," *Sage Open*, (July–September 2018): 8, https://doi.org/10.1177/2158244018785703.
11. Heather Devere, Kelli Te Maihāroa, Maui Solomon, and Maata Wharehoka, "Tides of Endurance: Indigenous Peace Traditions of Aotearoa New Zealand," *ab-Original: Journal of Indigenous Studies and First Nations and First Peoples' Cultures* 3, no. 1, (2019): 24, https://www.jstor.org/stable/10.5325.
12. Cappelli, "Standing with Standing Rock," 1.
13. Michelle Raheja, "Imagining Indigenous Digital Futures: An Afterword," *Studies in American Indian Literatures* 29, no. 1, (2017): 172–173.
14. Raheja, "Imagining Indigenous Digital Futures," 172.
15. The ACLU has compiled a list of 76 policing agencies contributing personnel to Standing Rock including the North Dakota National Guard. See, Thomas Dresslar, "How Many Law Enforcement Agencies does it take to Subdue a Peaceful Protest?" *American Civil Liberties Union*, November 30, 2016, https://www.aclu.org/blog/free-speech/rights-protesters/how-many-law-enforcement-agencies-does-it-take-subdue-peaceful?redirect=blog/speak-freely/how-many-law-enforcement-agencies-does-it-take-subdue-peaceful-protest.
16. TigerSwan, a clandestine security firm, was revealed to have been hired by Transfer Energy Partners to spy on the protesters and initiate paramilitary operations to dislodge protesters. See Alleen Brown, Will Parrish, Alice Speri, "Leaked Documents Reveal Counterterrorism Tactics used at Standing Rock to 'Defeat Pipeline Insurgencies'," *The Intercept*, May 27, 2017, https://theintercept.com/2017/05/27/leaked-documents-reveal-security-firms-counterterrorism-tactics-at-standing-rock-to-defeat-pipeline-insurgencies/.
17. Michael Edison Hayden, Catherine Thorbecke, and Evan Simon, "At least 2,000 Veterans Arrive at Standing Rock to Protest Dakota Pipeline," *ABC News*, December 5, 2016, https://abcnews.go.com/US/2000-veterans-arrive-standing-rock-protest-dakota-pipeline/story?id=43964136.
18. The New York City Stands with Standing Rock Collective, "#NoDAPL Syllabus Project," in *Standing with Standing Rock: Voices from the #NODAPL Movement*, eds. Nick Estes and Jaskrian Dhillon (Minneapolis: University of Minnesota Press, 2019), 303.
19. The New York City Stands with Standing Rock Collective, "#NoDAPL Syllabus Project," 302.
20. The New York City Stands with Standing Rock Collective, "#NoDAPL Syllabus Project," 303.
21. The New York City Stands with Standing Rock Collective, "#NoDAPL Syllabus Project," 303.
22. The syllabus in its pdf format is over 2,000 pages in length.
23. The first sit-ins were enacted by workers unions and then expanded into the civil rights movement, the most famous being the lunch-counter sit-in at a

Woolworths department store in Greensboro, North Carolina, by black students Ezell Blair Jr., David Richmond, Franklin McCain and Joseph McNeil.

24. David Myer Temin and Adam Dahl, "Narrating Historical Injustice: Political Responsibility and the Politics of Memory," *Politics Research Quarterly* 70, no. 4, (2017): 905, https://doi.org/10.1177/1065912917718636.
25. Ann M. Blair, *Too Much to Know: Managing Scholarly Information Before the Modern Age* (New Haven: Yale University Press, 2010), 3.
26. Temin and Dahl, "Narrating Historical Injustice," 905.
27. Zygmunt Bauman, "Education in the Liquid-Modern Setting," *Power and Education* 1, no. 2, (2009): 160, http://dx.doi.org/10.2304/power.2009.1.2.157.
28. Bauman, "Education in the Liquid-modern Setting," 160.
29. New York City Stands with Standing Rock, Timeline of Events, *#Standing Rock Syllabus*, 4, https://nycstandswithstandingrock.wordpress.com/standingrocksyllabus/.
30. New York City Stands with Standing Rock, Timeline of Events, 5.
31. Patrick Wolfe, "Settler Colonialism and the Elimination of the Native," *Journal of Genocide Research* 8, no. 4, (2006): 388, https://doi.org/10.1080/14623520601056240.
32. Melissa Gniadek, "The Times of Settler Colonialism," *Lateral: Journal of the Cultural Studies Association*, i. 6.1, (Spring 2017), https://doi.org/10.25158/L6.1.8.

7

#RAPECULTURESYLLABUS

I better use some Tic Tacs just in case I start kissing her. You know I'm automatically attracted to beautiful – I just start kissing them. It's like a magnet. Just kiss. I don't even wait. And when you're a star, they let you do it. You can do anything. Grab 'em by the pussy. You can do anything.[1]

The rape culture syllabus[2] emerged in the wake of Donald Trump's nomination as the preferred Republican candidate for the 2016 presidency. This nomination was in spite of the release of the Hollywood Tapes that recorded Donald Trump using predatory language. Trump dismissed these accusations by appealing to normative masculinity describing the language as 'locker-room talk' as if male spaces are separate from the consequences and realities of everyday life. In doing so, he reified a dissociative split that sustains patriarchal ways of being and thinking that simultaneously separates men from the consequences of social regulation and norms, and also validates a denial of male violence by suggesting, unlike other groups in society, that there is no connection between how a man speaks and his behaviour. This denial – of abuse, of predation, and the truth of what the words conveyed towards women – set the framework for Trump's success. This success is built as much upon the expectations and configurations of masculinity as it is on the capacity to reconfigure 'the real'. For women, whose words have frequently been dismissed and denied, particularly when it comes to formal reporting of sexual assault and harassment, it was confirmation of an ongoing and entrenched patriarchy that celebrates the exploitation of women in a world where one in five women have experienced rape in their lifetime.[3] The tolerance of these dismissals would not last, and the endurance of women would bubble over into an eruption of anger.

While 'Me Too' had existed for over a decade as an activist movement,[4] it began to trend on Twitter in the aftermath of a 2017 *The New York Times* report by Jodi Kantor and Megan Twohey exposing sexual assault accusations against Hollywood movie producer Harvey Weinstein. Actress Alyssa Milano used her Twitter account to ask for similar stories of sexual harassment from her followers using the hashtag #MeToo 10 days after *The New York Times* report. Within 24 hours, the phrase MeToo and its variants were tweeted more than 500,000 times.[5] The sheer scale of this use spilled beyond Twitter, and the hashtag was deployed by '4.7 million people in over 12 million posts on Facebook'.[6] #MeToo came a year after the release of the Hollywood Access tapes and the electoral success of Donald Trump and conveyed a bubbling resentment against a continued normalisation of offensive and predatory behaviour towards women by men across all sectors of everyday life.

In response to Trump's predation and fuelled by the accusations against Bill Cosby and the trial of Brock Turner, Kelly Oxford had deployed Twitter to call for reports of women's experiences of their very first assaults – an achingly revelatory post in acknowledging that many women experienced multiple circumstances of predation and assault in their lives. There was no hashtag. Women simply replied to Oxford using the @ symbol in direct messaging. Her tweet was a simple request:

> Women: tweet me your first assaults. they aren't just stats. I'll go first:
>
> Old man on city bus grabs my 'pussy' and smiles at me. I'm 12.[7]

In response, Kelly Oxford activated women's collective memories of harassment and they deployed the hashtag #notokay to express solidarity. It was the enduring crisis of anger cultivated by the repressed truths of sexual predation that threatened to spill over into an 'eventual' moment that aligned in the #MeToo movement following the outing of Harvey Weinstein as a serial predator. This anger was productive in articulating the betrayal of resilience tropes that instead of asserting the importance of justice, encouraged women to tolerate and ignore routine abuse of power upon their bodies. A rape culture syllabus emerged as a way to build on the refusal of #notokay in revealing the repressed truths of rape culture, women bodies in space and the narratives that malign women within the everyday real. The syllabus deploys a feminist refusal to cultivate women's narratives as reactionary. Anger is tempered by radical thinking to open the space for an educated hope that is transformative. Dialogue is created in strategies of communal justice for both men and women in a rejection of the repressed truths of femininity and masculinity. It seeks an evental moment in double refusal where knowledge sets gendered identity free from power differentials.

Rape culture refers to the ways in which the sexual exploitation of women across social sectors including interpersonal relationships, popular representations and in spaces of work and leisure is not only crucial to the circulation of desire and social erotics but also essential to the construction of valid and valuable patriarchal masculinities. It also services a fear-based framework for understanding sexuality that is corrosive and crippling for both men and women. Rape culture is as much about male sexuality as women's and functions to codify men as dangerous by affirming the constant threat of male predation upon women's sexuality – even making it a 'prerequisite for patriarchy'.[8] The assumption that all men are dangerous due to the misogynist nature of patriarchy leads to the reactionary but facile #notallmen protest. #Notallmen is designed to stall any radical reinterpretation of the status quo, but also provides a springboard into the complexities of many of the contemporary terms seeking to make sense of the debates about power and sex, bodies and autonomy, law and representation that reaffirm a culture of contestation, sexual conflict and interpersonal violence. The circulation of 'toxic masculinity' as it has emerged through such debates is questionable in that it treats masculinity as an infection that must be treated and eradicated. #MeToo and #notokay centralise the ways heterosexual men have benefitted from a legal and social system that diminishes women's experience of harassment, does not believe their truths of reported rape and enshrines tolerance of abuse in the codification of 'good womanhood'. Women must be resilient in the face of corrosive and dangerous masculinity, enshrining the inability for women to change or intervene in bodily exploitation. What this means for an active and reactive understanding of rape culture and how we effectively contextualise sexual relations in these circumstances is challenged in the rape culture syllabus. Radical understandings of desiring and erotics are needed. Much of this current understanding, unfortunately, is mapped out in investigations into rape and sexual assault and the deployment of legal and law enforcement language to exclusion of other perspectives that complicate desire, objectification and sexual gratification.

It is important to understand that sexual assault is not exclusively 'something' that men do to women. It can infiltrate power structures in many insidious ways with victim and perpetrator not so clearly binarised or defined. Capitalism thrives on division and persecution, creating networks of desire that repeat and replicate in order to motivate consumer fetish. Consumer desire also operates primitively on bodies and through sexual interactions that are mediated through the simulations of consumption. The desires of the flesh are transposed onto objects to be desired, bought and consumed. The desires of the body are pathologised and displaced into the shops, where substitutes can be purchased, disposed of and repurchased in a never-ending cycle of desiring and always delayed satisfaction. We never come face to face with our real desires to help develop healthy modalities for processing them. They are only ever replicated and simulated. Cauterised rape narratives as indicative of deviant sexuality are enfolded into gender relations that most obviously reassert women as victims and men as perpetrators. These archetypal stories are cultivated through a series of myths about rape that enact specific and narrow types of masculinity and femininity. The dualities of 'male force and female reluctance were an integral part of the construction of "normal" sexuality in the eighteenth and nineteenth centuries'[9] and remain imprinted on sexual relations today. In order to be constructed as a 'good' and virtuous woman, resistance to sex is presented as essential to preserving honour and virtue. Feminism has since intervened in such nonsense but has also revealed more complex meanings by affirming a liberated woman as a sexually open and voracious one, free to accept sexual congress wherever and whenever she sees fit without sacrificing her virtue. However, while it frees women from the supposed 'shame' of sexual desire, it also reaffirms old assertions that deep down even if a woman says no, she really means yes. All that is needed to unlock consensual heterosexual sex is for a man to insist. Such assertions have percolated throughout understandings of rape and the rape culture that supports particular invasions and incursions on bodies in sexual exploitation. In legal terms, a woman who did not want to have sex 'had to fight him physically – and hard – otherwise, he could assume that she was simply a "real woman"'[10] amplifying her demure resistance to his overtures. Sexual relations were peppered with 'the idea that violence was welcome'[11] and for rape to be proven a woman had to show 'not only that she'd physically resisted her assailant, but that she had kept up the resistance constantly throughout'.[12] In neoliberal capitalism, aggressions and competitions in all sectors of the social as well as the intimate are affirmed. Steve Hall refers to this as a *pseudo-pacification process*.[13] In this argument, the physical aggressions of the Late Middle Ages are subdued by the civilising process of liberal capitalism. Hall argues that the aggressions are just redirected into consumerism and the supports for economic expansion. Capitalism affirms inequity so it can continue to fuel desire – pseudo-desire for stuff to replace real fulfilment and sustenance. Male heterosexual desire enters into crisis by being stripped of the corrosive narratives that once reified aggression, pursuit and insistence as normal sexual interaction, but now lack progressive and nuanced narratives to replace these tropes. More precisely, these narratives now offer up flaccid alternatives. Deviancy is normalised due to this failure of language as well as a hobbling of desire into caricatures of yearning. Male heterosexual sex continues to be based on appropriation, ownership and taking. The erect penis as the centre of all pleasures leads to a pathology of permissiveness in asserting and inserting a simulacra of pleasure into public spaces and onto women's bodies. Consent can no longer be assumed but to ask permission implies a weakness in male prowess.

In mainstream pornography, all women want heterosexual penetrative sex. This desire is depicted by insertion of the penis into all orifices. The s(t)imulated women enthuse for it. No matter what the male in the video does with his penis, the woman exclaims in delight and in pleasure, urging for more. The man also does not have to do anything to secure her pleasure. Female enjoyment is not predicated on him activating desire in her except that he is in possession of a penis. They only need the presence and the penetration to be aroused. Despite these absurdities, porn is not the problem. Porn is just one site of sexual representation among many. The problem is that men very often learn their sexual literacies first and foremost through pornography. Michael Flood reported in 2010 that in Australia, 73% of 16- and 17-year-old boys 'had watched an X-rated video'.[14] Other research shows that 'by age 17, an overwhelming majority of boys (93%) and girls (62%) have been exposed to pornography'[15] and that it 'is a significant source of sex education for young people'.[16] It is important to note that young men learn as much about their own performance as the sexual behaviour of women in these videos. There is a plethora of pornography that present diverse sexual literacies and even educate men on pleasure (for a woman or other sexual partner); however, for the cheap climax offered by porn, there is usually a short narrative setup (depending on fetish) followed by close-up penetrative action, in many circumstances emphasising the violence and aggression of insertion and sexual exertion. There is little emphasis on foreplay unless it is for the man, contraception is rarely present and consent is avoided by either the gleeful enthusiasm of the woman (or women) or the manipulation and trickery of the man presented as part of his sexual skill (and the naïveté/stupidity of women to fall for his tricks). This ongoing depiction of sex as unequal and exploitative is an example of how 'our cultural narratives turn penises into omnipotent weapons with just one aim: to enter the vulnerable inner space of women, who – being defenceless – are at the mercy of this assault'.[17] In heterosexual pornography, the women may sometimes be depicted as active agents, but mostly they are presented at least as naïve and at most as eager enthusiasts for the exploitations enacted upon their bodies.

In rape culture, women's bodies are always and unconditionally available for the pleasure of men. Rape culture involves the dynamic suppression of consent, enacting its (forceful) denial by assuming the sexual availability of women in public spaces and the implicit assumption of access in private ones. Rape culture is a coherence of 'multiple pervasive issues that allow rape and sexual assault to be excused, legitimised and viewed as inevitable'.[18] In an era where consent is being discussed more overtly as a result of feminist interventions into sexual relations and the configurations of women as sexual subjects instead of sexual objects, women's right to bodily autonomy gains greater traction in how pleasure and desire manifest on their embodied surfaces. Previously sex was 'depicted as something that men *give* to women ... or take from them'.[19] This complication of the sexual narrative between men and women unsettles the pleasurable exchanges and the desiring tropes in heterosexuality. The power structures that condition women's availability and, therefore, muted consent are destabilised. It is a trembling of the sexual narratives of both men and women.

Rape culture exists between the act of sexual contact and the deployment of consent. There are men who assault women randomly and in public by groping, leering, following and harassing. The growing visibility of these moments is a result of women talking about it more often through #NotOkay and #MeToo. The behaviour they identify is the result of a variety of clichéd configurations including predatory masculinity where men think they have the right to women's bodies, deviant sexualities that gain pleasure from the risk of getting away with illicit contact and the shame and discomfort it evokes in the women, as well as men who do it because they can in a legal system that often reluctantly prosecutes sexual assault. Such reluctance and leeway for male predators is exampled by the Brock Turner case where in sentencing the judge expressed concern over the impact of a jail term on his life,[20] and even Jeffrey Epstein who in 2007 was permitted day release for up to 12 hours a day 6 days a week as a part of a plea deal for charges related to soliciting a minor for prostitution.[21] With the leniency of legal systems unwilling or unable to deploy rigorous insight into the complexities of sexual assault, consent and criminality, it is easy to see the trajectories that support sexual deviancy as normal in masculinity. The continuity of this behaviour exists across social stratification. It was the predations of Bill Clinton that paved the way for Donald Trump when he responded (honestly) to queries about his extramarital affair with Monica Lewinsky while he was president with: 'because I could'.[22] A response that speaks to the impunity with which male heterosexuality is permitted to act in public. This is a pathology that is embedded not in individual psyches, but culturally confirming an authority existing in 'the real' and its consequences. Capitalism demands desiring tropes that mask 'lack' throughout everyday consciousness and manifests that absence upon exploitable bodies. This 'lack' presents itself as a crisis that must be sedated. Daily 'mundane' abuses cultivate and encode the victimisation of women so they are available to men clasping a pathological masculinity that needs women to be diminished to bolster their power. The success of the feminist movement has meant that patriarchy is unsettled. Men are destabilised in the coherence of their connection to patriarchy and a corrosion of their social power manifests in personal crises that find purchase on women's bodies as a site for navigating social impotency. Because 'violence is capable of destroying power, but unable to create it',[23] sexual assaults are the repertoire of insecure men. Accelerated capitalism has dislodged men from their traditional centres of power, so sexual assertion tethered to the seductions of consumer culture is all they have left. This does not make men victims, but it does complicate their relationship to predation, sexual potency and power. In advancing hedonism and nihilism, capitalism requires exploitation of objects as well as subjects. Women's bodies are frequently 'consumed' – in advertising, film and television, and even on the street. In this 'hyper-modern era where symbolism, desire and *jouissance* have been conflated',[24] men are encouraged 'to feel guilty when [they] fail to take advantage of the opportunities for the hedonistic delights that abound in consumer culture'.[25] This 'reoriented superego injunction to enjoy'[26] that is at the centre of accelerated capitalism defines a culture-wide pursuit of pleasure. For men, who are used to patriarchy operating *for* them, its new alignment with the hedonism of permissibility in consumer capitalism makes sex an ideal space for the pursuit of personal joy and pleasure. It requires that pleasure be pursued insistently, encouraging predation as well as victimisation, consent as well as its denial. Capitalism does not want men recognising their vulnerability as wage earners, providers, consumers, partners or men. As a desiring framework, capitalism cultivates a constant state of wanting, needing, fulfilling but never quite satisfying. It is distracting. This lack has also resulted in a displacement of empathy and 'the less empathy, and especially empathy with oneself, a society allows, the less its members can respect other people's boundaries'.[27] Seeing women as objects of their desires rather than subjects with desires of their own, men seek to colonise women's pleasure, making them fit within male heterosexual desiring frameworks to fill the desiring lack consumer capitalism advances.

#NotOkay emerged out of the heritage of #MeToo in response to the predatory narrative advanced by Donald Trump and specifically to express dismay at the GOP in supporting his nomination as the Republican candidate for president. #NotOkay is a refusal. It is a rejection of the continued practices of those in power ignoring the real experiences of women in their everyday lives while advancing a skewed rendering of male experiences of 'the real' as something to which they are outside, excluded and unaccountable to. #NotOkay is a refusal to be dominated. In the statement accompanying the launch of the Rape Culture Syllabus in October 2016, the author Laura Ciolkowski cites the Republican response to Trump's remarks.

> *Afterward in the GOP spin room, Alabama Senator Jeff Sessions staunchly defended his ally, insisting, contrary to the Department of Justice's definition, that grabbing a woman's genitals without her consent was not sexual assault.* [28]

The denial of consent structures a pathological perspective on human rights, bodily autonomy and social agency. The everyday assaults and abuses some women experience are part of a deviant and perverse rendering of desire, bodies and power and should not be advanced as a normal part of accelerated late capitalism. #NotOkay and #MeToo demonstrate that these are not aberrations or deviance, they are a normal part of how women are encountering male (hetero)sexuality. The deployment of the language by Donald Trump served to assert the normality of predation for women as well as men as predators. Women responded by refusing this narrative. The hashtag opened the space for this refusal. This was not activism against Trump, but much larger in its intent. #NotOkay is a refusal of the sexualised status quo. It is a refusal to consent to ongoing pathologies of desire. It is a pre-empted refusal and a reclamation of consent located within the subject of desire rather than the desiring subject.

Ciolkowski begins the Rape Culture Syllabus with Sharon Block's *Rape and Sexual Power in Early America* published in 2006. Block maps her terrain as the 'gap between the personal coercion of sex and the public classification of rape'.[29] Consent is in tension as if it can be bartered and traded, rather than freely given or withheld. The discussion immediately asserts the rocky terrain of legal definitions for rape that have been anxiously upheld as well as poorly framed and, therefore, largely ineffectual in defending women's sexual rights. The struggles over gender, race and space in early America is the setting for the struggles over these relationships. Importantly, she demonstrates that these sexual (non)rights were tethered to economic and social conditions and cogently affirms that 'normative practices of consensual sex are understood only when we know where the category of consensual sex ended and that of rape began'. This first reading on the Rape Culture Syllabus list demonstrates that consent is negotiated and exchanged in complexities that affirm nuanced power structures. Heterosexual men have been able to move within these structures to secure as well as stipulate sexual encounters. The messiness of these interactions and the power differentials that impacted upon the uneven negotiations are situated in contrast to the refusal of #NotOkay that claim ownership over those anxious moments and assert the autonomy of women's bodies in critical consciousness. The everyday real of women is spotlighted as embedded in an embodied crisis that is constantly policed and navigated. The play of meanings around rape and sexual coercion may be complex but consent is simple. #NotOkay is a response to the tangling complexities of rape culture that threaten to blur the boundaries of women's agency and is a refusal to permit permeability around those meanings.

The syllabus interrogates the range and types of legal definitions and social conditions that have conspired to diminish women's experiences of rape, by both diluting and extending the test for consent, as well as removing it entirely as was seen fit by those in power to secure the continued access to women's bodies and their compliance within heterosexual reproductive family units. Ciolkowski has data-mined archives for first-hand accounts, commentaries and obscure ephemera to give a comprehensive sense of the writing on rape and sexual assault from a variety of perspectives. This interdisciplinary approach to the syllabus includes reading from Angela Davis to Maya Angelou as well as Susan Bronwmiller's groundbreaking book *Against Our Will*. There are accounts of male rape, the codification of slut politics, the relationships between slavery, lynching and sexual mutilation, sex workers, marital rape, queer and gay male sexual assault, #blacklivesmatter, college culture and masculinity, rape as warfare, incarceration, false reporting and sexual violence in detention, and finishing with creative works on rape including art, sculpture, multimedia and performance art.

The syllabus ends with Susan Williams' 1992 *Irresistible* sculpture. Depicting a woman lying prone on her side. She is inscribed with text.

> *THANKS FOR THE BEER. LOVE IS FORGIVING. IF YOU DON'T CARE ABOUT YOURSELF, HOW DO YOU EXPECT OTHERS TO – YOU DUMB BITCH. I DIDN'T DO THAT. HAVE YOU BEEN SEEING SOMEONE – HUH SLUT. I THINK YOU LIKE IT MOM. LOOK WHAT YOU MADE ME DO. THE NO.1 CAUSE OF INJURY TO WOMEN IS BATTERY (MEN) 'COURSE NO ONE ASKS WHAT THE WOMAN DID. HE'S UNDER A LOT OF ——————————— OH DO. SO. UPTIGHT. CAN YOU FIND SOMETHING TO RAM IN HER MOUTH? WE DON'T KNOW IF SHE ENJOYED IT OR NOT. THIS CASE REMAINS A MYSTERY.*[30]

The sculpture conveys the surfaces of a woman's body upon which consent and coercion is visualised. These surfaces are bruised and beaten. The language written on her body negates her consent. It removes her body from her agency entirely making the story by which her body is understood separate from her self, dancing on legalities and co-opting her identity. Making her mean something only in relation to the placating or rendering of masculine heterosexual desire. Pleasure is not present. There is only abuse in an effort to coerce or take her consent. She has no recourse to refuse because the narrative keeps changing and she is bound by this Gordian Knot of meaning, shaming her, denying her agency and making her into an object for desire rather than a subject with desire. The 1992 sculpture continues to resonate as it demonstrates how the language used to contain and control women has barely changed even though it morphs to suit the power structures at play. In 2019, Australian radio 'shock-jock' Alan Jones suggested that Australian Prime Minister Scott Morrison should 'shove a sock down the throat'[31] of New Zealand Prime Minister Jacinta Arden. Reducing women to mere orifices to be invaded in order to control and contain their ability to speak to their own agency (offer or deny consent) remains a core trope in sexual politics. #NotOkay stands as a refusal – to shut down the debate about consent and affirm its boundaries, refusing the narrative flexibility that threatens to undermine women's sexual rights in the complex dance of honour, shame, obligation, desire and anxiety that infiltrate debates about consent and coercion. The Rape Culture Syllabus opens this debate, starting from a place of refusal, and in engaging with scholarship about women's, men's, raced, classed and trans bodies, new ways of thinking about domination is visualised through the consent commentary. In refusing to engage in the narratives that insert women into rape culture and instead identifying the ways these stories instil or deny consent, the syllabus offers a framework for #NotOkay to be actionable, resonant and interventionist.

NOTES

1. Donald Trump, "Transcript: Donald Trump's Taped Comments about Women," *The New York Times*, October 8, 2016, https://www.nytimes.com/2016/10/08/us/donald-trump-tape-transcript.html.
2. It is important to note that the Rape Culture Syllabus is not crowd-sourced but instead has one author and curator, Laura Ciolkowski Associate Director of the Institute for Research on Women, Gender and Sexuality at Columbia University. The syllabus is hosted on the *Public Books* site. http://www.publicbooks.org/rape-culture-syllabus/.

3. Katherine W. Bogen, Kaitlyn K. Bleiweiss, Nykia R. Leach and Lindsay M. Orchowski, "#MeToo: Disclosure and Response to Sexual Victimization on Twitter," *Journal of Interpersonal Violence*, (2019): 2, https://doi.org/10.1177/0886260519851211.
4. "Me Too" was initiated in 2006 by activist Tarana Burke on MySpace. See https://metoomvmt.org/about/.
5. Bogen, Bleiweiss, Leach, and Orchowski, "#MeToo," 5.
6. Bogen, Bleiweiss, Leach, and Orchowski, "#MeToo," 5.
7. Kelly Oxford, (@kellyoxford) "Women: tweet me your first assaults," *Twitter*, October 8, 2016, 7:48 a.m., https://twitter.com/kellyoxford/status/784541062119456769.
8. Mithu Sanyal, *Rape: From Lucretia to #MeToo* (London: Verso, 2019), p. 25.
9. Sanyal, *Rape*, 9.
10. Sanyal, *Rape*, 11.
11. Sanyal, *Rape*, 11.
12. Sanyal, *Rape*, 11.
13. Steve Hall, "The Socioeconomic Function of Evil," *The Sociological Review* 62, s. 2, (2014): 13, https://doi.org/10.1111/1467-954X.12189.
14. Michael Flood, "Young Men Using Porn," in *Everyday Pornography*, ed. Karen Boyle (London: Routledge, 2010), 165.
15. Chyng Sun, Ana Bridges, Jennifer A. Johnson, and Matthew B. Ezzell, "Pornography and the Male Sexual Script: An Analysis of Consumption and Sexual Relations," *Archives of Sexual Behaviour* i. 45, (2016): 994, http://dx.doi.org/10.1007/s10508-016-0744-0.
16. Sun, Bridges, Johnson, and Ezzell, "Pornography and the Male Sexual Script," 984.
17. Sanyal, *Rape*, 115.
18. Alexa Dodge, "Digitizing Rape Culture: Online Sexual Violence and the Power of the Digital Photograph," *Crime, Media and Culture*, (2015): 3, https://doi.org/10.1177/1741659015601173.
19. Sanyal, *Rape*, 18.
20. Sam Levin, "Stanford Sexual Assault: Read the Full Text of the Judge's Controversial Decision," *The Guardian*, June 15, 2016, https://www.theguardian.com/us-news/2016/jun/14/stanford-sexual-assault-read-sentence-judge-aaron-persky.
21. Liam Stack, "U.S. Opens Inquiry into Handling of Jeffrey Epstein's Sex Abuse Case," *The New York Times*, February 6, 2019, https://www.nytimes.com/2019/02/06/us/fbi-jeffrey-epstein.html.
22. David Hancock, 'Clinton cheated "Because I could"' *CBS News*, June 16, 2004, https://www.cbsnews.com/news/clinton-cheated-because-i-could-16-06-2004/.
23. Sanyal, *Rape*, 117.
24. Simon Winlow and Steve Hall, "Retaliate First: Memory, Humiliation and Male Violence," *Crime, Media, Culture* 5, no. 3, (2009): 290, https://doi.org/10.1177/1741659009349243.
25. Winlow and Hall, "Retaliate First," 289–290.
26. Winlow and Hall, "Retaliate First," 291.
27. Sanyal, *Rape*, 113.

28. Laura Ciolkowski, Rape Culture Syllabus, *Public Books*, October 15, 2016, http://www.publicbooks.org/rape-culture-syllabus/.
29. Sharon Block, *Sexual power in Early America* (Williamsburg: University of North Carolina Press, 2006), 2.
30. Susan Williams, *Irresistible*, 1992, http://images.huffingtonpost.com/2012-04-12-TL46.jpg.
31. Amanda Meade, "Alan Jones's Radio Show Loses Hundreds of Advertisers since Jacinta Arden Storm," *The Guardian*, November 25, 2019, https://www.theguardian.com/media/2019/nov/25/alan-joness-radio-show-loses-hundreds-of-advertisers-since-jacinda-ardern-storm.

8

#SANCTUARYSYLLABUS

Newspapers and television networks across the country reported last week that President Trump had signed an executive order compelling meat-processing plants to remain open even as their employees test positive for the coronavirus in droves. Meat and poultry executives quickly praised the president's action, while unions condemned Trump's order for prioritising industry interests above workers' lives. Predictably, Senate Republicans applauded the President, while Sen. Bernie Sanders (I-Vt.) and Congressional Democrats derided Trump's move. The nonprofit Environmental Working Group warned that Trump's order could be a 'death sentence' for workers.

Lost amid all of this was the fact that Trump's order, which appeared on the White House website late Tuesday, does not actually order meat-processing plants to reopen. Indeed, it does not order the meat-processing plants to do anything. And although the president had told reporters Tuesday that his order would 'solve any liability problems' that plants might face with respect to lawsuits arising from covid-19 exposures, the order does not do that either. Far from a death warrant, it is a paper-thin proclamation with limited legal effect.[1]

Meat-packing plants in the United States have been at the centre of previous political posturing. As one of the most prevalent employers of migrant workers (documented and undocumented), these sites have been at the crux of debates about mobility, citizenship and worker's rights. The packing plants rely heavily on the liminal status of many of the migrant workers in their employ leveraging their precarity by paying low wages with some reports of

$12.50 USD or less per hour. There are also reported declines in working conditions and negligence around worker safety in these plants.[2]

This has created a 'double-bind', where migrant workers are leveraged for the exploitations of agricultural and industrial labour including meat-packing and crop-picking as well as construction, forming a cheap workforce for their employers who are 'resolutely nonunion and pay workers as little as $10 an hour for dangerous, demanding physical labor'.[3] This exploitation sits awkwardly against the border-protection rhetoric that demonises migrant workers and marginalises their role in the United States' economy. Scholars have gone so far to argue that the workers are actually essential to neoliberal economies.

> *Unauthorized workers are foundational to neoliberal systems of production, and central to the emergence of a new working class in North America. The status of illegality creates social illegitimacy around the workers' personhood, facilitating employers' exploitation serving the system of flexible capital accumulation and disciplining workers to perform their role as a subordinated class.*[4]

The struggles around the personhood of migrants are particularly acute for the undocumented, where swinging and sweeping policy changes from Obama to Trump administrations have had profound effects on the everyday real of these people. Meat-packing plants were spotlighted in 2019 when they were subject to one of the largest immigration raids in United States' history. Across Mississippi, ICE (Immigration and Customs Enforcement) targeted four poultry processing plants.[5] About 680 workers were arrested, detained and deported as part of Trump's hard-line approach to migration policies.

In the public posturing enacted to assert power and control over systems of governance that are not within his reach, Donald Trump was using the liminality of migrant workers and repressed truths around their role in the economy to craft a real conducive to his desired outcomes. In trying to out-flank resistance and dominate the national debate, Trump's posturing was played out on terrain upon which he wields little power and in playing into that power he attempted to claim, the post-truth paradigm of fake news augmented Trump's failure to lead and reified his position. As argued by Hemel,

> *The president's assertions of legal authority, like his off-the-cuff medical advice, often have little basis in reality. But our responses*

> to the president's statements do matter because we can transform his imaginations into facts on the ground.⁶

It is in these spaces of a critical and negotiated 'real' that the case study of the Sanctuary Campus operates – between the assertions and actualities of power and how these are understood and manifested in the everyday real.

President Obama was nicknamed 'Deporter in Chief' in accusation of amplified numbers of undocumented removals during his presidency. In Obama's first term, 2.5 million people were deported largely because of changes in the terminology defining 'deportation' to include immigrants detained immediately at the border which were previously recorded as 'voluntary returns'.⁷,⁸ In fact, numbers show marked reductions in deportations under Obama than compared with Presidents Bush and Clinton.⁹ Over two terms, Obama deported just over 5 million people, whereas Bush was almost double that with over 10 million (during his two terms) and Clinton even higher in his two terms with over 12 million. Under Obama's presidency, the enforcement of immigration law was proportionate with hardened criminals targeted, and terrorists and national security threats taking precedence. This was enabled by a presidential directive to exercise 'prosecutorial discretion' by ICE in its actions.¹⁰ Under Trump, this proportionate response evaporated. Donald Trump's 2016 election was built upon a draconian border policy framework, a 'wholesale roundup and deportation of illegals'¹¹ and promises to 'build a wall'. Soon after his inauguration, Donald Trump signed an executive order on 'Enhancing Public Safety in the Interior of the United States' which approved the deportation of all illegals. While this binary approach to legal and illegal residents served to secure conservative votes and smooth fears in a time of financial, climate and social collapse, it has once again used migrant bodies as the space to pummel out tensions and anxieties about the future, about wealth and prosperity, fairness, crime and deviance.

What is particularly perverse about this approach is its betrayal of public trust. Frustrated with ongoing Congressional gridlock regarding illegal or undocumented migrants who were living in the United States because of their arrival as children with their parents, in 2012, President Obama signed an executive order implementing Deferred Action for Childhood Arrivals (DACA). This order allows people who arrived illegally with their parents to live and work lawfully in the United States subject to a number of strict provisions including being resident in the United States for more than five years, and currently be in school, be a high-school graduate, hold a high-school completion certification or be an honourably discharged veteran of the United States army.¹² DACA effectively removes the threat of deportation and allows applicants to apply for work permits and driver's licenses. The programme received close to one million applications.[13] In September 2017, Donald Trump repealed DACA. These undocumented young people have effectively outed themselves to immigration officials. They are currently in a position of precarity, as legal challenges are mounted to preserve DACA and prevent widespread deportations. If Trump is successful, ICE will have photographic and biometric data to track and evict DACA recipients. It is a massive betrayal of public trust and hope. It is the framework in which the sanctuary movement has gained increasing visibility. Sanctuary cities in particular have been subject to overt and direct threats by President Trump because they operate in spaces of ambivalence – where the clean, cold and objective, legal and illegal, documented and undocumented, criminal and citizen tropes cannot be so clearly conjured and contained and where anxieties about contemporary constructs of citizenry threaten to boil over. Sanctuary cities call attention to the nuances and niches of public power, revealing a negotiated real where an educated hope is permitted to flourish and double refusal can germinate.

Sanctuary cities and campuses recognise migratory complexity and reify disobedience. Since inauguration, Trump has been threatening sanctuary cities with defunding because of the threat they pose to his authority to impose conservative and changeable neoliberal rights upon the undocumented. In these city spaces and now spilling onto a sanctuary campus movement, the evolving complexities of changing citizenship patterns are called to attention. The contemporary crises of opportunity, employment, mobility and safety are written into these spaces and the citizenship performances that are enacted. For some time, the status of 'citizen' as a coherent category attached to the nation-state has been under attack, not only with increasing global mobility of the displaced with global estimates of 244 million international migrants, but also with a steady 'citizenship gradation'.[14] This is the decline of clear binaries between 'citizens' and 'noncitizens' or border crossers. Where once, citizenship merged with modern nation-states intact and unassailable, it is now subjected to a variety of gradations. For example, in many 'western' contexts, any citizen suspected of being a terrorist can be stripped of their rights and removed without their consent, depending on national policy. Wonders and Jones refer to this as 'the multiplication of citizenship' where 'western nations have proliferated distinct packages of citizenship rights and limitations, from guest worker programs to the treatment of terrorist suspects to felony disenfranchisement'.[15] These categories compose a sliding scale of belonging, access and rights management beneficial to the crafted precarity of the neoliberal state. It is within this framework that the tenacity and tenuousness of citizenship and the performative power of belonging are spotlighted. Neoliberal efforts to destabilise the tether between rights and responsibilities anchored within citizenship models of the social contract reframe the workplace as the dominant mediator of access to services and sustainability. With the ongoing decline of the welfare state and the demonisation of government assistance recipients, the workplace is the domain to demonstrate self-reliance and leverage inclusion. These tensions play out on the border where the straining space for visualising social justice shrinks to the right to work and access to employment.

> *Much of the work of contemporary bordering seeks to produce the subjectivity of the 'illegal' – the non-person who is unworthy of rights – as well as to valorize the shrinking rights held by those still privileged enough to access citizenship.*[16]

In the global precarity of accelerated capitalism, it is in the interests of power structures to detain, reframe and demonise so-called 'illegals' in their threat to working opportunities, thereby also focusing attention onto the one place remaining for rigorous rights management by citizens – the workplace. Struggling over the right to work is an essential and convenient battleground for accelerated capitalism. The seductions of an inside/outside binary constructed at the border masks the sustained precarity citizenship rights are currently subject to. The delivery of government services is now so thoroughly undermined that the very status of citizen is being called into question to dislodge the tether between rights and responsibilities within a contemporary democracy. Welfare and service provision is displaced onto the workplace and into the individual. The objective of these highly strung social debates about 'illegals' and 'aliens' is to simultaneously draw attention to and mask the precarity of global neoliberal economies of exchange. The emphasis placed on the 'undocumented' within this debate offers special space for consideration. The function of 'documents' in migration is to leverage and regulate access to citizenship, to rights and to assistance.

Documents, filed formally and embedded within a materially objective bureaucracy of archival verification, are essential tools of the modern nation-state and the constructs of citizenry. European formations of citizenship were based on the rights of property ownership and as such were restricted to those imbued with the autonomy and authority to 'own' – slaves, women, land and those who lived on that land (Indigenous peoples). The textual systems of writing composed a truth structure that is hierarchical and authoritative; 'a transparent, portable and durable communicative technology capable of recording and translating fleeting social transactions into taxable and legible evidence of fact and reality'.[17] This is in effort to produce 'the fiction of the sovereign's irreducible and unfalsifiable existence'.[18] In the act of bestowing legitimacy onto the subject of the document, the sovereign authority asserts and affirms their own legitimacy. To possess documents is to exist in a democracy, to acknowledge its authority and to enable its legitimacy. Birth certificate, register of schooling, tax file number and social security are ways of legitimating identity and verifying existence. Documents register democratic rights and responsibilities. They can also be a register for persecution and terror as has been evidenced in times of crisis and conflict. Documentation and categorisation has been used to mark particular ethnicities and populations as abject and outside the nation-state. In each case, the function of 'documents' is to enact the 'state's power as guarantor of the written word.'[19] Through this written word is a guaranteed relationship to the sovereign, even if it is restricted, curtailed and corrosive. These relationships are mediated through the body – through scribing and stamping paper documents to create a 'papereality'[20] and through the definitions of what types of bodies are permitted access to these documental repertoires. Migrants at the border serve as a fulcrum point where these actions gain visibility. If 'the agenda of full citizenship is to reclaim rights (property rights) *over* [the] body',[21] undocumented migrants effectively surrender their bodily rights to the employer in exchange for a wage because without full existence and acknowledgement by the nation-state, they cannot leverage the right to a proper wage. Their body as property becomes the surface upon which they are rendered abject and criminal by discourses that define their mobility as wage theft and upon which citizen advocates and allies wage war to reclaim bodily autonomy in the mobility tropes of modern global economies, human dignity and rights. These tenuous and changing frameworks for understanding and crafting citizenship in a neoliberal global economy have profound impact upon what it means to be 'undocumented'. The complexity of these intersections has resulted in a range of social movements designed to question and critique the established notions of citizenry. With the currently estimated 11 million undocumented people currently living in the United States, these movements are not singular nor new, but work within established complexities of border management, human rights, resistance and collective action.[22]

    The contemporary sanctuary movement has its origins in the 1980s in the United States with border churches providing shelter and safety to the refugees fleeing crisis in El Salvador. Commonly conveyed origins however extend to biblical times where sanctuary could be claimed by people fleeing interclan violence. Sanctuary functioned as a 'safety-valve' – a way to provide respite from ongoing clan-war and blood-feuds of this period. A person could claim sanctuary even if they had committed a crime to provide a temporary respite from the cycle of vengeance killings. Once provided, the refugee could not leave the sanctuary city, but could craft out a life within its walls. More detailed histories show 'sanctuary has variously been associated with Christianity, Islam, Judaism, Buddhism, Baha'i, Sikhism and Hinduism in different contexts for thousands of years'.[23] It is a large and diverse movement that has many chapters. While sanctuary began in churches in the United States, it now encompasses entire cities.

Sanctuary cities provide refuge from the bureaucracies of neoliberal globalisation and operate on tenuous and tremulous terrain in-between spaces of policy and legality by mediating the subject's relationship to the state.

> *Throughout history, churches and the concept of sanctuary have filled important gaps in individuals' lives, which their relationships with the state – whether lordly, liberal or bureaucratically welfaristic – have not or could not fill. Such gap filling has been variously a welcome supplement to state welfare activities, a source of conflict with state policies allocating resources and ordering social relations, and an escape valve for domestic conflicts concerning political, social and legal issues.*[24]

Currently there are nearly 500 sanctuary cities in the United States that offer respite, food, shelter and safety to fleeing populations as well as individuals.[25] The contemporary sanctuary movement in the United States has accelerated at the cusp of Donald Trump's election into the presidency. They have endured overt threats by the administration seeking to limit the potency and currency of such cities in their disobedience to federal authority because of the ambivalence by which they view and enact decrees and edicts emanating from the office of the President.

There is no agreed upon definition of what a sanctuary city is and no clear consistency in approaches between regions or districts. It merely refers to an intent by a city and its authoritative structures to not freely offer up details of any potentially undocumented residents in their region to ICE without a warrant.

> *In most sanctuary and welcoming cities, policy directives state that local law enforcement officials are prohibited from inquiring about immigration status and need not alert federal officials about the immigration status of detained individuals. In many sanctuary cities, those without legal papers are permitted to work, receive educational services and obtain drivers' licenses.*[26]

This 'disobedience' to federal anti-immigration laws and the persecution of the undocumented is encased in the legal structures of the US system where 'nothing in federal law requires localities to enforce federal immigration laws'.[27] In response to this resistance, Trump has threatened to defund states with sanctuary cities. The Executive Order: Enhancing Public Safety in the Interior of the United States, issued January 25, 2017, affirms

> ...that jurisdictions that wilfully refuse to comply with 8 U.S.C 1373 [the law that prohibits local and state governments enacting laws that limit communication about immigration or citizenship status to the Department of Homeland Security] are not eligible to receive Federal grants.[28]

The Federal Court of Appeals upheld the District Court decision that this order is unconstitutional. The states have reasserted their right to offer sanctuary. This order operates in the terrain of obfuscation and ignorance. It assumes an authority the Federal government does not have, and it operated in tenuous territory in the assumptions made about legality and lawfulness.

> The executive order authorises DHS to designate 'sanctuary jurisdictions', without providing any definitions of the term, but does not immediately strip funding from 'sanctuary cities'. Nor does it clarify which federal funding sources could be denied since it exempts funding cuts for law-enforcement purposes.[29]

This order sought to railroad legislation into effect without due care for terms, consequences and outcomes. Instead, it was a strong-arm tactic designed to threaten and frighten based on ambiguity and raw assertion of power. It did not even bother with messy definitions. It confirmed a narrowing conservative bias about common sense and the collective assumption of meaning (about the law, about sanctuary and its purpose). A critically reflexive unpacking of that knowledge requires accountability and a deployment of authority that is nuanced. It is in this environment and with the model of the sanctuary cities that the sanctuary campus emerged to also offer protection and assistance to undocumented students. Sanctuary campuses form on university and college property to assist and protect the undocumented students that attend. Like the sanctuary city, the sanctuary campus pledges to not offer any details of undocumented students to ICE without a warrant.

The campus sanctuary movement connects to the church-based sanctuary movement by appealing to ideals above and beyond the legalities of nation-states. While churches appealed to a higher order of morality, divinity and charity, the campus sanctuary movement has anchored their intentions to the secular realm of human rights and dignity, specifically the right to an education. Mirroring its original designation, the sanctuary campus has no cohesive definition, but 'similar to sanctuary cities, colleges and universities that establish sanctuary campus status also face threats of defunding from legislators'.[30] Sanctuary campuses operate in ambiguous, in-between legal spaces where it remains crime to 'harbor or shield from detection' undocumented people.[31] The repeal of DACA has significant consequences for the sanctuary campus movement. As a pared-down effort to bring the Dreamer Act to realisation, DACA was aimed at offering educational opportunities to undocumented students. While Plyler v Doe in 1982 established that 'states could not deny students free public education based on immigration status', the same freedom was not applied to higher education.[32] DACA was an attempt to open up trajectories into higher education for these students who invariably had to take other options once they left the public schooling system. The sanctuary campus movement is an intervention into the DACA repeal in an effort to shield undocumented students from the betrayal that saw them offer up their undocumented status only to have it be used to criminalise and deport them.

Numbers of the undocumented in the United States have been in decline. Studies have also shown 'that improving social and economic conditions in sending countries could lead to a substantial decline in the undocumented population'.[33] In 2010, outside of Texas and California, New York had the largest undocumented population. From 2010 to 2018, that population has seen large declines of 25%. There were almost one million undocumented in New York in 2010. By 2018, that had declined to 684,000.[34] In this radically shifting landscape, the New York University (NYU) Sanctuary Coalition emerged in 2017 in direct response to the President of NYU Andrew Hamilton pledging not to hand over the details of undocumented students but refusing to deploy the sanctuary campus label. The formation of the Coalition is significant because Hamilton's reiteration of the University's policies was not a refusal. The reluctance to claim or assert the sanctuary campus label was a sign that the university hierarchy was situating itself within its already established parameters of operation – which would not put undocumented students at risk and would deploy many of the principles of the sanctuary campus – but was not a statement of refusal. The NYU Sanctuary Coalition codified this absence of refusal as a continued betrayal of the undocumented by allowing the narratives of legal and illegal to remain untested and unchallenged. In its position as a private university, its funding was not directly under threat of Trump's now defunct executive order.

Hamilton affirmed the position of the university in a rigorous public engagement process. He stated that current policies will stand, and as such there was no need to declare the university a sanctuary. On January 30, 2017, he wrote on the NYU website:

> It is hard not to see this latest development in the context of undocumented members of our community, whose status has also been the subject of much debate in Washington. I wrote to you in November about the steps we were taking to support them, but let me reiterate the key ones:
>
> - We will not permit federal officials on campus to gather information about immigrants in our community absent a subpoena or similar legal order;
>
> - Our Public Safety Officers do not and will not ask about the immigration status of members of the NYU community, nor will they voluntarily share such information with law enforcement;
>
> - We will vigorously uphold the privacy protections granted our students by federal law; and
>
> - The University's scholarship assistance to non-US citizens, which is independent of federal financial aid programs, will carry on regardless of changes to immigration policies.[35]

The NYU Sanctuary responded on their website in the frequently asked questions proportion, declaring the importance of sanctuary as solidarity:

> President Hamilton has stated that NYU will not be a Sanctuary Campus. We believe that the ever-growing assaults on members the NYU community should make him reconsider his initial decision. In these dangerous and uncertain times, NYU must rise to the challenge and make an unambiguous statement regarding our opposition to discriminatory and isolationist policies that harm the democratic values of both the United States and the university. Declaring ourselves a Sanctuary Campus would show the world that NYU rejects the politics of isolationism and fear. Moreover, as the flagship university in one of the most diverse and dynamic cities in the world, NYU has a special responsibility to show courage and leadership when it comes to standing with the vulnerable communities that make New York City so strong. History will judge NYU harshly if the administration fails to offer a clear and strong response during this unprecedented political times.[36]

The NYU Sanctuary Coalition mobilised its staff and resources to create a network of concerned and capable allies to provide resources for undocumented students and to facilitate matrices of refusal. They situated this action within the rigors and ethics of research and academic freedom codifying the university as a space where these principles must be upheld. Their website provides links to assistance from mobilising individuals who feel they can provide a safe place to travel advice, legal advice, understanding immigration policies, community action, lists of organisations, educational courses and events. Most notably, by the end of 2017, the Sanctuary Syllabus appeared on *Public Books* authored by the NYU Sanctuary Coalition.[37] It was not crowd-sourced but composed by the academic staff and students of the Coalition. A #sanctuarysyllabushashtag exists on Twitter but was not used specifically to gather suggestions for the syllabus, but rather to direct interested parties to the *Public Books* site. The introduction to the syllabus foregrounds the importance of refusal.

> *In the months since President Trump has attempted two more versions of the travel ban and announced the repeal of the Obama-era Deferred Action for Childhood Arrival (DACA) policy, stripping rights to work and study from 800,000 young people. The spectacular scenes of detention and border enforcement at the airports brought to light the intersecting roles of war, law, policing and racism in the current situation. But protesters transformed these spaces of control and surveillance into grounds for civil disobedience and creativity, manifesting the power of the public to demand and create sanctuary.*[38]

The syllabus is constructed as a toolbox for refusal with a declarative structure that enables readers to situate themselves within the network of action that the Coalition constructs. There are 14 weeks to the syllabus. Week one is labelled as a demand: 'Sanctuary Now!' The remaining weeks provide a scaffold for the political, social and educational importance of the refusals associated with sanctuary. Each week provides links to actual tools and the policies that motivate the sanctuary movement. This syllabus is about praxis. Sanctuary demands action. Refusal is a beginning with the process of revealing repressed truths to access in the everyday real an ongoing process. It is in the act of refusing that political intervention can be made while also demonstrating the solidarity in educated hope that offers a pathway into and out of the politics of double refusal. The syllabus and its interventions cannot be effective if not grounded in an information and knowledge scaffold that is acutely tapped into the changeable nature of law, politics, rights and justice. The spaces in which sanctuary cities and campuses declare themselves are in the complexities of variable and mobile public policy and law, attitudes and interest, as well as hard facts and ethical obligations. Sanctuary campuses are a refusal, and the syllabus provides the knowledge scaffold that refracts and accompanies, shapes and changes the action that can be offered by those seeking to mobilise educated hope in a time where refugees and the undocumented are seen as parasitic on the established national wealth of affluent countries. Sanctuary and the sanctuary syllabus is an effort to humanise and bring compassion and comfort into a debate that insists of demonising refugees and the undocumented as exploiters of the good will of others. It confirms precarity as a normalised subjectivity or archetype of the neoliberal condition and brings the complexity of knowing needed to unpack, decompress and denormalise this perspective as a deployment of the refusal to dominate. The syllabus offers the knowledge scaffold to support refusal and to provide the real-world tools to explore the borders to legal ramifications as they bump up against moral and ethical responsibilities in the defence of human rights, and the possibilities of hope in the shifting mobilities of citizenship and the ways in which documents, authority and scholarly rigor are massaged by the rhetoric and interests of those in power. The syllabus is a refusal to accept unethical government policy and a call to action into consciousness via radical thinking. It is a pedagogy of promise. It is the refusal of injustice in demonstrating not just that the university is an ally in informing and protecting students, but that there is a refusal of brutal forms of oppression with a call to solidarity and hope in action born out of knowledge in social history, the nuances of navigating state and federal law, the rights and responsibilities of citizens and how mobility, crisis and endurance intersect to create dignity for all human life. It is action grounded in knowledge, educated hope and double refusal.

NOTES

1. Daniel Hemel, "No, Trump Didn't Order Meat-processing Plants to Reopen: The President Likes to Claim Powers He Doesn't Really Have. We Don't Have to Go along with It," *The Washington Post*, May 4, 2020, https://www.washingtonpost.com/outlook/2020/05/04/trump-meat-processing-order/.
2. Human Rights Watch, *"When We're Dead and Buried, Our Bones Will Keep Hurting": Workers' Rights Under Threat in US Meat and Poultry Plants*, (2019), https://www.hrw.org/sites/default/files/report_pdf/us0919_web.pdf.
3. Lance Compa, "Migrant Workers in the United States: Connecting Domestic Law with International Labor Standards," *Chicago-Kent Law Review* 92, no. 1, (2017): 215, https://scholarship.kentlaw.iit.edu/cklawreview/vol92/iss1/9.
4. Miranda Cady Hallett, "Labor, Discipline, and Resistance: Transnational Migrant Workers 'On the Line'" *Journal of Working-Class Studies* 2, no. 1,

(2017): 25, https://workingclassstudiesjournal.files.wordpress.com/2016/06/jwcs-vol-2-issue-1-june-2017-hallett1.pdf.
5. It is important to note that ICE do not detain and separate parents from children at the US border. This is within the operational purview of Customs and Border Patrol.
6. Daniel Hemel, "No, Trump Didn't Order Meat-processing Plants to Re-open"
7. Yana Kunichoff, "The New Sanctuary Movement," *In These Times*, (June 2017): 16.
8. Glenn M. Ricketts, "The Campus Sanctuary Movement," *Acad. Quest.* 32, (2019): 87, https://doi.org/10.1007/s12129-018-9767-4.
9. See Muzaffar Chishti, Sarah Pierce and Jessica Bolter, "The Obama Record on Deportations: Deporter in Chief or Not?" *Migration Policy Institute*, January 26, 2017, https://www.migrationpolicy.org/article/obama-record-deportations-deporter-chief-or-not.
10. John Morton, "Exercising Prosecutorial Discretion Consistent with the Civil Immigration Enforcement Priorities of the Agency for the Apprehensions, Detention and Removal of Aliens," (memo), US Department of Homeland Security, https://www.ice.gov/doclib/secure-communities/pdf/prosecutorial-discretion-memo.pdf.
11. Ricketts, "The Campus Sanctuary Movement," 81.
12. Brian Harper, Brendan O'Boyle and Paola Nagovitch, "Explainer: What is DACA?" *Americas Society Council of the Americas*, December 5, 2019, https://www.as-coa.org/articles/explainer-what-daca.
13. Ed Pilkington, "Dreamers's New Risk after Daca: US Could Use Their Personal Data to Target Them," *The Guardian*, September 6, 2017, https://www.theguardian.com/us-news/2017/sep/05/daca-dreamers-personal-data-undocumented-immigrants.
14. Nancy A. Wonders and Lynn C. Jones, "Doing and Undoing Borders: The Multiplication of Citizenship, Citizenship Performances, and Migration as Social Movement," *Theoretical Criminology* 23, no. 2, (2019): 137, https://doi.org/10.1177/1362480618802297.
15. Wonders and Jones, "Doing and Undoing Borders," 139.
16. Wonders and Jones, "Doing and Undoing Borders," 142.
17. Shrimoyee Nandini Ghosh, "'Not Worth the Paper It's Written On': Stamp Paper Documents and the Life of Law in India," *Contributions to Indian Sociology* 53, no. 1, (2019): 21, https://doi.org/10.1177/0069966718810566.
18. Ghosh, "'Not Worth the Paper It's Written On,'" 21.
19. Ghosh, "'Not Worth the Paper It's Written On,'" 21.
20. Ghosh, "'Not Worth the Paper It's Written On,'" 23.
21. Carol Lee Bacchi and Chris Beasley, "Citizen Bodies: Is Embodied Citizenship a Contradiction in Terms?" *Critical Social Policy* 22, no. 2, (2002): 329.
22. Jeffrey S. Passel and D'Vera Cohn, "U.S. Unauthorized Immigrant Total Dips to Lowest Level in a Decade," *Pew Research Center*, November 27, 2018, https://www.pewresearch.org/hispanic/2018/11/27/u-s-unauthorized-immigrant-total-dips-to-lowest-level-in-a-decade/.
23. Jennifer J. Bagelman, *Sanctuary City: A Suspended state* (New York: Palgrave Macmillan, 2016), 20.

24. Sophie H. Pirie, "The Origins of a Political Trial: The Sanctuary Movement and Political Justice," *Yale Journal of Law and the Humanities* 2, no. 2, (1990): 387.
25. Wonders and Jones, "Doing and Undoing Borders," 146.
26. Wonders and Jones "Doing and Undoing Borders," 146.
27. American Immigration Council, Summary of Executive Order "Enhancing Public Safety in the Interior of the United States", May 19, 2017, 2, https://www.americanimmigrationcouncil.org/sites/default/files/research/summary_of_executive_order_enhancing_public_safety_in_the_interior_of_the_united_states.pdf.
28. The White House, Executive Order: Enhancing Public Safety in the Interior of the United States, January 25, 2017, Sec 9, clause (a), https://www.whitehouse.gov/presidential-actions/executive-order-enhancing-public-safety-interior-united-states/.
29. American Immigration Council, Summary of Executive Order "Enhancing Public Safety in the Interior of the United States," May 19, 2017, https://www.americanimmigrationcouncil.org/sites/default/files/research/summary_of_executive_order_enhancing_public_safety_in_the_interior_of_the_united_states.pdf.
30. Natasha Newman, "A Place to Call Home: Defining the Legal Significance of the Sanctuary Campus Movement," *Columbia Journal of Race and Law* 8, no. 1, (2018): 135–136.
31. Newman, "A Place to Call Home," 141.
32. Jeremy Peña, "Undocumented Students: History and Implications for Higher Education," *Journal of Hispanic Higher Education*, (2019): 2, https://doi.org/10.1177/1538192719860482.
33. Robert Warren, "Reverse Migration to Mexico Led to US Undocumented Population Decline: 2010 to 2018," *Journal on Migration and Human Security* 8, no. 1, (2020): 34, https://doi.org/10.1177/2331502420906125.
34. Warren, "Reverse Migration," 37.
35. Andrew Hamilton, "A Message from NYU President Andrew Hamilton about the Recent Executive Order on Immigration," January 30, 2017, *New York University* Website, https://www.nyu.edu/about/news-publications/news/2017/january/a-message-from-nyu-president-andrew-hamilton-about-the-recent-ex.html.
36. NYU Sanctuary, Frequently Asked Questions, accessed March 2, 2020, http://www.nyusanctuary.org/faq/.
37. NYU Sanctuary, "Sanctuary Syllabus," *Public Books*, May 12, 2017, http://www.publicbooks.org/sanctuary-syllabus/.
38. NYU Sanctuary, "Sanctuary Syllabus."

9

#BLACKDISABLEDWOMANSYLLABUS

There is a familiar news-reportage trope involving people with disability. These involve stories that are actually about able-bodied people and how nice they are to people with disabilities. You can find videos on YouTube of the high-school basketball, football or baseball team letting the student with disability play and make the touch-down, goal or score with crowds of their peers cheering them on. They may even let this person make the winning shot if the team has a far enough lead to be secure of the win. In 2018, the Australian media (along with many other global media outlets) reported a 'kindhearted barber' giving a disabled man a haircut in the street because his wheelchair could not fit in the shop.[1] The story was not about accessibility and how a society might advocate for greater inclusion and universally designed public and private areas. Instead it was about the barber and how nice he was to go out of his way for a disabled person. The story affirms the distribution of charity from abled to disabled. In February 2020, a local media story in Australia was headlined: 'Surf Lifesavers Hailed as Heroes after Granting 96-year-old's Humble Wish.'[2] At the beach, the lifesavers helped the elderly man, who uses a walker, to get from the car park, across the sand, to the water's edge. Again, the reportage was not about making beaches more accessible, but about the heroics of able-bodied people when they help 'the disabled'.

These types of stories are labelled 'inspiration porn'. Assigned to Stella Young, the phrase describes 'the "ableist gaze," which is when a person with disability is "seen" through the eyes of someone without disability' and in that perspective is 'used to highlight the lack of power experienced by people with disability in cultural representation' by constructing their everyday 'real' as condescendingly 'special' when they are living their lives in an everyday normality.[3] Young recounts the story of a member of her local community wishing to nominate her for an achievement award and her parents rightly pointing out that she 'hadn't actually achieved anything'.[4] She was merely living her everyday life. There was nothing 'inspiring' about her living literacies and to define her as inspirational is to diminish the everyday real within which people with disability live. These stories are designed to make able-bodied people feel good because of the contrast between the 'disadvantaged' disabled person and the divine generosity and gifting of the able-bodied population who 'helps' them. This charitable discourse is designed to affirm the disposability and dismissal of people with disability in any context in which they are not enabling an able-bodied person's self-esteem. These attitudes reaffirm 'compulsory able-bodiedness'.[5] This social and emotional role is tethered to a construction of disability as a pitying state – that disabled people are only granted value on the criteria by which able-bodied people can leverage the meanings, moments and memories that are harvested in the reification of a disabled object in contrast to able-bodied subject. Ego, charity, gifting and condescension are the cornerstones of this type of interaction. Denial of human status and diminishment of cogency within public spaces plague able-bodied relationships to people with disabilities. This asserts that people with disability are not full members of the social framework. As such, these structures do not have to acknowledge, accommodate or change anything to improve accessibility and affirm self-determination for people with disability. Disempowerment and disadvantage are the natural states of people with disability and the reification of eugenics debates confirms their role as the sub-human – worthy of pity but not empowerment.

The *10 Daily* story involving the barber cutting the disabled man's hair in the street demonstrated one rare moment of insight into the ways in which people with disability enter the representational terrain. The news outlet revisited the story after receiving complaints from disability activists and acknowledged their problematic reportage. They reaffirmed that 'this story should have been told differently',[6] acknowledging the ableism of the initial report. They recontextualised the narrative and instead of situating it as a charitable act, quoted Jordan Steele-John, an Australian Senator, that indeed, it would have been discrimination for the barber to have denied service to the disabled man whether his wheelchair could access his shop or not. Steele-John's narrative contextualised the experience of disability within a human rights framework and legal debate normalising full human status for the man in the wheelchair and asserting his legal rights to service. This denial of charity activates universal design and accessibility as a fundamental human right for all members of society. Narratives continue to circulate that define people with disability as non-human and not subject to the same rights and responsibilities as everyone else. It is this fundamental perversion of citizenship and humanism that demands refusal.

In the *Pedagogy of the Oppressed*, Paolo Freire argues for humanism as the antidote to oppression. Marginalising structures seek to subtract humanity, and groups that abide by the meaning systems imposed upon them this way can only fall into nihilism when what is right and good and solid is stripped away by the narcissism of the neo-liberal consciousness that configures humans in terms of their exchange value. For people with disability, the status of human is frequently denied, either implicitly in social interactions or legally in policy and legislation. Resistance is about agitating for change. This change is commonly constructed as recognition, diversity and inclusion. Groups struggling to land onto the terrain of relevance within neo-liberal capitalism claim visibility so they can be accounted for in the trajectories of representation. Freire argues the fundamentally corrosive nature of capitalism is its power to morph and change without ever being dislodged. It simply accommodates more identities, groups, perspectives, as long as it can turn it into a new market, for new consumer identities to grow within. He argues that it 'is the great humanistic and historical task of the oppressed: to liberate themselves and their oppressors as well'.[7] For this to occur, the double bind of capitalism must be provoked to understand the injustice that 'to have the continued opportunity to express their "generosity," the oppressors must perpetuate injustice as well'.[8] Just like the deployment of inspiration porn that helps able-bodied people feel good about the dispossession of people with disability, capitalism normalises abuse, degradation and persecution to convince those subject to that abuse that it will end only with full entry into the bountiful and abundant spaces of capitalism. Presenting itself as the prize, resistance struggles and strains against the limits of capitalism, but never rewrites the terrain upon which these encounters occur.

Within critical disability studies, bodies in binaries are troubled with all common sense meaning systems connected to corporeality destabilised, questioned and reconfigured. The trajectories of embodied understandings are redefined by evolving through medicalised models of disability which configure the disabled body as a defect that can either be fixed by medical intervention or masked through technology 'allowing people to "overcome" their impairments'.[9] These ways of thinking are asserted as civilised, modern and enlightened approaches to disability that did not hide or institutionalise individuals or configure them as defective or deviant. In the social model, the medicalised reliance on masking, changing and reconfiguring the disabled body, deploying ableist assertions about what normal body and neurological function is upon people with disability is challenged. The causal relationship between 'impairment' and 'disability' is deconstructed and shifts the burden of change onto social meaning systems and structures rather than physical interventions onto the body from within medicalised knowledges that seek to retrofit a disabled body into the semblance of an able-bodied one. In the social model 'disability [is] the effect of an environment hostile to some bodies and not to others, requiring advances in social justice rather than medicine'.[10] A person is disabled when they encounter stairs not because they are in a wheelchair but because the society in which they live does not and will not accommodate a variety of mobilities and deploy a universally designed urban environment to provide access and assistance for everyone. It is the attitudes and thinking structures that disable first and foremost, the body is only secondary to this disenfranchisement. It is within the context of an evolving and radicalised social model of disability that Vilissa Thompson via her website Ramp Your Voice launched the Black Disabled Woman Syllabus coinciding with the hashtag #Disabilitytoowhite, as a point of radical resistance to the unacknowledged labour of disabled activists who often bear the burden of having to educate nondisabled people about disability rights. #Disabilitytoowhite was coined by Thompson in response to Alice Wong calling out representation of disability in an article about fashion, beauty and disability in online magazine *XOJane* (a now defunct website). #Disabilitytoowhite mobilises arguments that not only are representations of people with disability rare and fraught with clichés, untruths and problematic constructs but also representations of people of colour with disability are conspicuously absent. This has real consequences for the amplified dangers and threats people of colour with a disability face in everyday life.

Thompson created the hashtag in response to Wong's critique of the prevalence of whiteness in disability representation. It was a consequence of this intervention that Thompson recounts the uptick in requests for information coming through her activist website Ramp Your Voice.[11] These requests appeared to be asking about the focus on women of colour. In frustration, Thompson created the Black Disabled Woman Syllabus.

> *I created the syllabus as a way of being a reference point so that if people had questions, I could be like, 'Here. Here's a starting point for you to educate yourself and not ask me to do the labor so that you would understand why black disabled women [unclear] and the black disabled experience as a whole matters and why you need to be more conscious of the way that you talk about disability, the way that you bring about disability topics in conferences and panels, etc'. So it was my way of not having to be pressured to do the labor that*

people fail to go to Google for. So I figured just put something together that mattered and that has been widely shared within the past two years, particularly within academia circles, having people really put their bodies of work and it would be a reference point in adding to what existed.[12]

The intellectual and emotional labour of people with disability to educate able-bodied people is a burden. The work that people with disability have done to make change in rights and regulations are now taken for granted but masked in many benefits able-bodied people assume. The contributions of people with disability to social justice, urban planning, medical science and a whole gamut of intellectual, social, economic and legal frameworks are consistently and intentionally wiped from the collective memory. Accessibility and inclusion laws which benefit all people are often hard-fought disability rights. The Black Disabled Woman Syllabus and #Disabilitytoowhite is a refusal to be wiped out of contemporary debates about representation and social justice. The overarching ableism 'is not just a matter of ignorance or negative attitudes towards disabled people; it is a trajectory of perfection, a deep way of thinking about bodies, wholeness, permeability and how certain clusters of people are *enabled* via valued entitlements'.[13] This includes the denial of the contributions of people with disability to the knowledge, rights and intellectual repertoires of the everyday real. The 'abled imaginary'[14] is an unconsciousness network of meanings that circulate as common sense, across all sectors of 'the real' to limit and define 'human ontologies and corporealities'[15] marginalising disabled knowledge, experiences and contributions. The work of re-educating ableists is frequently borne by people with disability. Formal educational institutions are inadequate in their engagement and deployment not only of people with disability in professional positions as educators and trainers but also in the knowledge cache that their radical thinking strategies produce in an educated hope. To deny the labour in justice, advocacy and critical thought ignores the refusal and radical rethink of the relationships between knowledge, scholarship and 'the real' that people with disability deploy every day. This repressed truth of disability labour – as a site for education, intervention and affirmation of marginalising ideologies about ability and normality – slumbers within its evental potentiality.

The emotional labour assigned to people with disability is considerable and constant. Because of the assumptions of the able-bodied, people with disability must continuously educate how their behaviour, in its assumptions about assistance and helping people with disability, is actually disempowering. This most often involves assuming the type of assistance needed by the person with disability instead of asking. As a consequence, there are many and grave breaches of privacy and personal autonomy, daily endured by people with disabilities. Some single out the taking control of a person's wheelchair without consent as an example of a grotesque assumption and assertion of able-bodied assistance. Disability blogger Nina-Marie Butler demonstrates how this type of behaviour and assumptions about acceptable interactions with people with disability is encoded as normal among the abled population.

> *So here I am, outside work waiting for my taxi when a woman who happened to be going past, stopped to ask if I needed any help. I thanked her, said I was all-good and wished her a good evening. But she did not move.*
>
> *'I wish I could get away with one of those', she said, pointing to my walking frame. I just smiled. She obviously took this as a good sign and went on, 'what's wrong with your legs?' She asked. 'They're wonky', I replied. 'I can see that', she said. 'What about the feet?' She enquired. 'They're wonky too', I answered.*
>
> *Now I really wanted her to go away, but of course she did not. Instead she stood there staring at my bare legs (I was wearing a skirt), then down to my boot-clad feet. 'Can I see them'" She asked. I said no. Apparently, this was unacceptable, as she seemed very affronted as she marched off.*
>
> *Astoundingly, that was not the first time I have been asked to remove my shoes and socks in public so a curious person can inspect my feet. It happened at work once years ago too. When I declined to go barefoot in the middle of the office, the reaction was much the same.*
>
> *To some, the request to remove shoes may not be a big one, but to me it is. We all have aspects of our bodies that we would prefer not to flaunt, and this is mine. In addition, really, why should I? My disability, no matter how visible does not make me a public spectacle.*
>
> *What you are asking (especially when no one else is doing it, or I do not know you) is the equivalent of 'show us your tits', and I am not about to do that either.*[16]

These sense-making structures extend into the everyday experiences of people with disability. Such approaches have been spotlighted in the current unfolding COVID-19 situation, where the physical isolation and social distancing being advocated are often just not feasible for some people with disability who require everyday intimate care. This is compounded by rhetoric casually advancing that 'ordinary' people need not worry because only the elderly and those with underlying conditions should be concerned about dying from coronavirus. Most profoundly, people with disability are acutely aware that because of their 'deviant' and less than human status, they will most likely be denied treatment if they fall ill. This is not an alarmist perspective. In April 2020, news outlets reported the 'heart-warming' moment a 34-year-old man with Down syndrome was reunited with his family having beaten coronavirus.[17] This report also included information that he was initially placed in palliative care and was not expected to survive.[18] For disability activists, this exemplifies the casual way in which people with disability are expected to meet death – without intervention and without care that would be extended to any other 34-year-old. Further evidence of this cavalier connection between disability and death can be tracked in reports of an increase in the number of Do Not Resuscitate orders being either imposed upon or strongly advised for people with disability during the coronavirus crisis.[19] Such narratives operate within what Campbell calls *'abyssal thinking'* where like Freire's trope of oppressors perpetuating injustice so they have a platform upon which to perform their 'generosity', the invisible acts 'as the foundation of the visible category'.[20] The consequence is that when the invisible demands visibility, it often is irruptive. The anger of people with disability is palpable. Refusals are radicalised.

> *Shout out to every exhausted cripple who is simultaneously battling to coordinate supports and safety, fighting rising panic and terror, fighting fucked up policy and operational decisions, listening to every abled asshole living casually drop ableist statements or be outright hostile while watching a steady flow of eugenics and ableism slide by their mentions you're doing eight times the emotional load that those people are.*
>
> *It's okay to feel like you're feeling.*
>
> *To the ableds with the casual survival of the fittest narratives just fucking stop. And imagine what it's like having this flow over you like a fresh wave of scalding acid over your already burned skin, over and over. Just stop.*[21]

It is within this highly volatile and ongoing assault on the rights of people with disability to live, let alone ensure appropriate accessibility to public and private spaces, that the debates about media representation take up such importance. This is not equivalent to refraining from representing black people as drug dealers and gang bangers, or people from the Middle East as terrorists. Certainly, these are serious clichés that are damaging, often lethal and need intervention. Yet, the meanings around these identities are already mobile, and there are real-life interactions that belie these mediated constructs. For people with disability who have spent much of their history locked up in institutions or euthanised at or before birth, their very presence is a nexus for crisis and complexity at the foundations of what is understood as 'human'. Their visibility in the public sphere is life-saving.

Representation is never enough. To advocate for greater or 'more authentic' representation of people with disability simply repeats the pastiches of identity politics grasping for space within the public consciousness and confirms Freire's lament about complicity in power structures. Representation can offer short-term eruptions into sense-making, and it does expand the repertoire of images and simulations people draw upon as they navigate through their daily lives and negotiate diversity. It can make a huge difference in the lives of people with disability who are absent from public visibility. The presence of a person with a prosthetic or with autism in the popular media creates a normalising framework for different bodies and experiences. Greater visibility within the media is significant, but it does not make policy and it does not render consciousness complex. Instead clichés are often extended, not eliminated. Representations are only ever representations – they always exist in the space of simulacra, never quite interfacing with the real but instead standing in for it. In Baudrillardian simulacra, these images are valuable and powerful. Advocating for diverse representations in the media is an important sector of disability activism. Seeing oneself in the space of popular entertainment serves to centralise and normalise an embodiment, a neurotype or perspective in visible, leisured and interactive spaces to de-emphasise strangeness. For people with disability, this easing of threat, danger, fear and disgust of different bodies is transformative in their lives where bodily boundaries are tenuous, leading to the fragile purchase on the realm of 'human' in response to ableist narratives. This fragility is a core trope in dominant entertainment narratives that frequently portray being disabled as worse than death. Films like *Me Before You* and *Million Dollar Baby* convey these tropes and contribute to a culture where people with disability are pitied and pathologised. It is considered 'normal' and right that a woman should terminate a pregnancy if disability is detected in the foetus. These are ingrained and deeply entrenched perspectives about bodies, humanity and disability as deviance complexly woven into common sense understandings about human rights, ethics and human 'nature'. Fiona Campbell has argued that this is akin to being 'subaltern, existing in very defined, vexed and precarious cultural spaces and realities'.[22] Disability activists argue that diversity in representation can undermine simplistic assertions about disabled experiences and provide a pathway towards productive interactions across all societal sectors. This can help to dislodge the deeply entwined perspectives on what it means to be human that remain tethered to linear embodiment and predictable neurotypes. But, it can only go so far in articulating the 'limits of neo-liberal parameters of tolerance that display ambivalence and reversal'.[23] These limits never spill over into a full rejection and overturning of the parameters of capitalism as the container for the perverse, eugenic humanism that reifies ableist approaches to 'the real'. It only repeats a cycle of people with disability campaigning for more visibility within the system built upon their invisibility. Instead, new ways of understanding the relationships articulated in the process of differentiating ableism and disability is needed. Campbell argues for both categories to be seen as a 'becoming', 'as a *practice*, as a *process* which is in aporia' or paradox.[24] The infinite negotiations that can take place in this mobility system is ultimately *en*abling in terms of agile thinking and conceiving in 'the real', opening up possibilities and potentialities.

When Vilissa Thompson created the Black Disabled Woman Syllabus, she referred to it as 'a living document'.[25] She anticipated it to be mobile and transformative not only just in terms of the practicalities of its curation in adding new materials according to changes over time and situational debate but also in terms of its conceptual articulations. The Syllabus is not just about advocating for greater representations of black disabled women in the popular media. It is a refusal – to do the emotional labour allocated to the invisible person with disability, for them to simply agitate for change without ever really disturbing the normative, ableist constructs that might make room for difference and diversity. It is a subversion of the system that presents able and disabled in a binary. The hashtag permits this mobile space by aligning competing and conflicting perspectives, ideas and ways of thinking to coexist, merge, divergent and contrast. It is a refusal to be wiped out of history and a denial of the dual spaces of dominated and domination. For people with disability, these are normalised tropes of interfacing with 'the real' that are imposed upon embodied types precisely in comparative work that elevates abled over disabled. Crucially, Freire called upon education to do the work of transformation in offering the tools to 'perceive the reality of oppression not as a closed world from which there is no exit, but as a limiting situation which they can transform'.[26] This can only happen in a refusal to regard 'the oppressed as an abstract categor'[27] as is facilitated in the bringing together of the hashtag syllabus in a mobile archive of knowing, being and doing.

> *Making 'real oppression more oppressive still by adding to it the realization of oppression' corresponds to the dialectical relation between the subjective and the objective. Only in this interdependence is an authentic praxis possible, without which it is impossible to resolve the oppressor-oppressed contradiction. To achieve this goal, the oppressed must confront reality critically, simultaneously objectifying and acting upon that reality.*[28]

For Freire, consciousness is not enough. It is only a beginning. By situating a continuum of knowledge, artefacts and outputs in a hashtag syllabus that is changeable and fluid, an authentic intervention in 'the real' becomes possible by presenting literacies, tools and praxis as possibilities for productive evental change. Importantly, the Black Disabled Woman Syllabus begins with '12 Important Reads for Revolutionary Black Women'. These books affirm the place and role of activism in education providing a toolbox of perspectives on changemaking that enfold around and through race, gender, regionality, violence, politics, class, crime and law. These texts are memoirs, scholarly, autobiographical, poetic, geopolitical, ethnographic and reflective. The scale of the material in this syllabus offers a wide-ranging macro-perspective on the interconnected ways in which 'normal' is maintained and sustained. By gathering these resources, it functions as a refusal to categorise and define what it means to be a Black Disabled Woman. While the resources themselves present a framework within which meaning is defined and shaped, the mobility and living nature of the syllabus facilitated by the hashtag means that categories can be conjured and crumbled. In affirmation of the actionable nature of this material and the importance of intervening, debating and critiquing, Thompson situates its pedagogical nature by affirming 'class is now in session'.[29] By deploying the language of discipline associated with pedagogy rather than the permissibilities of andragogy, Thompson is affirming the rigor associated with attempting to see a new 'real' which requires a radical and critical consciousness. Reading these materials without disciplined examination of your own perspectives is railed against by Thompson, and readers are urged to apply an inquiring mind.

It is only in this situation of radical thinking that a double refusal can be conjured. By examining the strategies by which an educated hope can transform resilience into endurance and open the possibilities for a critical interrogation of 'the real' in ways unhampered by the formulae of official narratives and perspectives, new opportunities present themselves. In the spaces of capitalism which seek to colonise all thought and squeeze out or appropriate all forms of resistance, the seductions of the double refusal remain potent in slipping into radical thinking that can liberate criticism and expertise from current discard. People with disabilities demonstrate a disobedient refusal to conjure the tropes of the abled to ask for entry into the domain of dispossession. This is the essence of the double refusal. It is transformative, difficult and sometimes dangerous.

NOTES

1. Jessica Dunne, 'Barber Cuts Hair in Street because Wheelchair Couldn't Fit into Shop', *10 Daily*, September 21, 2018, https://10daily.com.au/news/good-news/a180921ctd/barber-cuts-hair-in-street-because-wheelchair-couldnt-get-into-shop-20180921.
2. Jessica Galley, 'Surf Lifesavers Hailed as Heroes after Granting 96-year-old's Humble Wish', *Starts at 60*, 12 February, 2020, https://startsat60.com/discover/news/calounda-surf-life-saving-club-96-year-old-man-wish.
3. Katy Gagliardi, 'Facebook Captions: Kindness, or Inspiration Porn?' *MC Journal*, 20, no. 3, (2017), http://www.journal.media-culture.org.au/index.php/mcjournal/article/view/1258.
4. Stella Young, 'I'm Not Your Inspiration, Thank You Very Much', *Ted Talk*, June 9, 2014, https://www.youtube.com/watch?v=8K9Gg164Bsw.
5. Robert McRuer, 'Compulsory Able-Bodiedness and Queer/Disabled Existence', in *The Disability Studies Reader*, (second edition), ed. Lennard J. Davis (London: Routledge, 2006): 301–308.
6. Emma Brancatisano, 'Why This Story of a Barber's "Kind-Hearted Act" Should Have Been Done Differently', *10 Daily*, September 25, 2018, https://10daily.com.au/news/australia/a180924gjm/why-this-story-of-a-barbers-kind-hearted-act-should-have-been-done-differently-20180924.
7. Paulo Freire, *Pedagogy of The Oppressed*, (translated by Myra Bergman Ramos) (New York: Continuum, 2005), 44.
8. Freire, *Pedagogy of The Oppressed*, 44.
9. Deborah Lupton and Wendy Seymour, 'Technology, Selfhood and Physical Disability', *Social Science and Medicine* 50, no. 12, (2000): 168.
10. Tom Siebers, 'Disability in Theory: From Social Constructionism to the New Realism of the Body', in *The Disability Studies Reader*, (second edition), ed. Lennard Davis (New York: Routledge, 2006), 173.
11. Vilissa Thompson, *Ramp Your Voice*, accessed April 15, 2020, http://www.rampyourvoice.com/.
12. Vilissa Thompson, 'Supporting Black Women with #Disabilities with Vilissa Thompson', *Day in Washington: The Disability Podcast*, (transcript), http://dayinwashington.com/supporting-black-women-with-disabilities-with-vilissa-thompson/.
13. Fiona Kumari Campbell, 'Precision Ableism: A Studies in Ableism Approach to Developing Histories of Disability and Abledment', *Rethinking History* 23, no. 2, (2019): 146, https://doi.org/10.1080/13642529.2019.1607475.
14. Fiona Kumari Campbell, *Contours of Ableism: The Production of Disability and Abledness* (Houndmills: Palgrave Macmillan, 2009), 4.
15. Campbell, *Contours of Ableism*, 4.

16. Nina-Marie Butler, 'No, You Can Not See My Tits!' *Inner Musings of a Funny Looking Kid*, (Blog), March 26, 2019, https://ninimeany.wordpress.com/page/1/.
17. See 'Covid 19 coronavirus: Down Syndrome Man Given Hours to Live Reunites with Family after Beating Virus', *New Zealand Herald*, 20 April, 2020, https://www.nzherald.co.nz/world/news/article.cfm?c_id=2&objectid=12326119.
18. See Raven Saunt, 'Heartwarming Moment a Man with Down's Syndrome, 34, Who Was Given 24 Hours to Live Is Reunited with His Mother after Beating COVID19', *Daily Mail*, April 20th, 2020, https://www.dailymail.co.uk/news/article-8234729/Man-given-just-24-hours-live-contracting-coronavirus-reunited-mother.html.
19. Rebecca Thomas, '"Unprecedented" Number of DNR Orders for Learning Disability Patients', *HSJ*, April 25, 2020, https://www.hsj.co.uk/coronavirus/unprecedented-number-of-dnr-orders-for-learning-disabilities-patients/7027480.article?fbclid=IwAR3u2Qnj9XNnXwSD6sXWCY7Kh-bz7wyJcacrjHIOa3wGoJHgq3xBX_e_7h8.
20. Campbell, 'Precision Ableism', 143.
21. Samantha Connor, Facebook Post, April 2, 2020, 21:04 p.m., https://www.facebook.com/moondyne
22. Campbell, 'Precision Ableism', 142.
23. Campbell, 'Precision Ableism', 144.
24. Campbell, 'Precision Ableism', 145.
25. Vilissa Thompson, 'Black Disabled Woman Syllabus: A Compilation', *Ramp Your Voice*, May 5, 2016, http://www.rampyourvoice.com/?p=2421.
26. Freire, *Pedagogy of the Oppressed*, 47.
27. Freire, *Pedagogy of the Oppressed*, 50.
28. Freire, *Pedagogy of the Oppressed*, 51–52.
29. Thompson, 'Black Disabled Woman Syllabus'.

Conclusion

POPULAR PROVOCATIONS: #LEMONADESYLLABUS AND #COLINKAEPERNICKSYLLABUS

As the coronavirus crisis unfolded, universities became critical places for managing the potential spread of disease. Universities initially remained open, but when on 15 March Australian Prime Minister Scott Morrison announced that large gatherings of people were illegal, universities promptly began emptying their campuses, with varying urgency. Some immediately closed and offered financial support for all staff. Other campuses removed the students, kept staff and required libraries, cafeterias and study spaces to remain open. By 23 March most Australian universities had abruptly closed all face-to-face teaching and had pivoted to online learning. It was only in the aftermath of this decision that the cascading consequences for staff, students and the sector as a whole have become increasingly cataclysmic. In early April when the Prime Minster advised any visitors to Australia, including students on study visas to head home, it mapped out a potential future of crisis for Australian universities that rely on large numbers of international students for funding.[1]

There are currently over half a million international students enrolled in Australian higher education, the majority of which come from China.[2] In 2017 international students accounted for 23% of university revenue.[3] In 2020 six universities recorded that over half their revenue came from international students.[4] The increase in reliance on international student numbers has been a direct result of the decline in Australian government funding to the university sector. This retraction has been systematic and ongoing.

> *Total funding to universities under the CGS [Commonwealth Grant Scheme] grew by 59 per cent between 2009 and 2015, mainly as a consequence of substantial enrolment growth. However, in real (inflation-adjusted) terms, funding per university place grew by less than 1 per cent each year between 2009 and 2015.*[5]

With the abrupt pivot to off-campus modes, the retraction of international students, the coronavirus crisis has profound effects on the sector. Some commentators are predicting a loss of between AUD$3 and $4.5 billion for Australian universities.[6] More crucially, in the heart of the storm, universities have not been made eligible for emergency funding to support retention of workers during this period, and staff are reporting hiring freezes. This is especially significant for sessional employees. While statistics are hard to come by because casual staff are usually masked in university data, the Grattan Institute estimates that 'on a full-time-equivalent basis, casual staff are 23 per cent of the university academic workforce. On a headcount basis, casually-employed academics are probably a majority of the academic workforce'.[7] A hiring freeze means that contract renewal is now on hold. Most of these staff members will not be employed in the new teaching term leading to thousands of job losses. Experts are predicting up to 21,000 jobs will be lost within six months.[8] This is not just an Australian problem, with the United Kingdom and the United States also reporting a potential crisis in their sectors.

> *The American Council on Education believes revenues in higher education will decline by $23bn over the next academic year. In one survey this week, 57 per cent of university presidents said they planned to lay off staff. Half said they would merge or eliminate some programmes, while 64 per cent said that long-term financial viability was their most pressing issue. It's very likely we are about to see the hollowing out of America's university system.*[9]

These numbers track the economic value of education. There is less mapping the intellectual fallout of this crisis and what it means for the future. Ironically, by not standing their ground and advocating for their position as critical thinking centres essential to democracy, universities are now faced with massive defunding of both public and private funds. By not enacting a refusal to abide by neoliberal policies demanding they make a profit and thereby prove themselves economically valuable to the social framework, they have permitted the corrosion of public debate and have signed the death warrant for their institutions.

The diminishment of expertise is a complex denial for this institution, with it being the commodity on sale to students, while also affirming the relevance of university scholarship to 'real world' practicalities over and above abstract theories and nonsense thinking. The attacks on university funding have been accompanied by a rejection of scholarly knowledge with neoliberal conservative condescension to the lofty and the abstract. It is no coincidence that the humanities and social sciences are often singled out for their 'wastage' of public funds.

In 2018, Australian Education Minister Simon Birmingham directly interfered in the public review process for the delegation of research funds by vetoing AUD$4 million worth of grants. The projects vetoed were mostly humanities based and had already been approved by the Australia Research Council. They included topics such as: 'Writing the Struggle for Sioux Modernity', 'Soviet Cinema in Hollywood Before the Blacklist 1917–1950', 'Beauty and Ugliness as Persuasive Tools in Changing China's Gender Norms', 'Writing and the Literary Archive', 'A History of Australian Men's Dress', 'Post-Orientalist Arts of the Strait of Gibraltar', 'Music Heritage and Cultural Justice in the Post-Industrial Age' and 'Greening Media Sport'.

The blocking of funding for these projects is indicative of the disdain with which unconventional or unpopular thinking is viewed by conservative interests. Perceptions of projects that involve thought experiments or unpopular ways of knowing rub awkwardly against the value for money demanded of scholarly output in accelerated capitalist neoliberal economic thinking.[10] In the tensions between what is radical, what is resistance and what is refusal, the policing of knowledges that 'should' circulate within 'the real' takes shape along a specifically economic axis. Eruptions outside of and in between these frameworks are sites for anxiety. Popular culture is particularly provocative and can provide a bubbling cauldron of potentiality to both manifest and mute these eruptions. The dual sites of Beyoncé's *Lemonade* album and the Lemonade Syllabus[11] along with Colin Kaepernick's knee-taking rebellion during the national anthem at the third pre-season game of the NFL in 2016,[12] providing impetus for the Colin Kaepernick Syllabus,[13] render the complexities of popular culture in dialogue with what is known and how people know, disobedient ways of knowing, and the trivialisation of the everyday. These two sites, bouncing off and between black bodies and popular culture, provide a reckoning for how 'the real' is understood and negotiated via refusal.

Beyoncé released *Lemonade* in 2016. Labelled a 'visual album' the project is a combination of popular music, film, poetry and performance art. It was considered a radical departure for Beyoncé, configured as her least 'popularly' oriented work. The 'affective turn' of the album has been affirmed as an articulation of a double disaster.

> *Beyoncé links her personal disaster (her suspicion that her husband, Jay-Z, had been cheating on her) which motivated the production of the album, with contemporary political and social events and*

movements affecting the lives of black Americans, from Katrina to racial violence and #BlackLivesMatter.[14]

The album is codified as a homage to feminine rage, the American south and black womanhood as well as the devastations of Hurricane Katrina and Black Lives Matter. The visual performance accompanying the music is filled with potent imagery of southern-ness, tribal heritage, magic, sisterhood, anger and redemption. 'Beyoncé is Oshun, the Nigerian, Cuban and Brazilian orisha of sweet water, sexuality and creativity, whose generosity makes life worth living and whose wrath begins with rolling laughter that foreshadows disaster.'[15] This potency is punctuated within a careful repertoire Beyoncé and her husband deploy displaying masterful manipulation of the popular media in the management of their personal lives. Critics have accused the couple of leveraging their romance to craft a public persona to sell records. Both Beyoncé and Jay-Z are conscious of imagery. *Lemonade* is the opening instalment of a trilogy for the couple, followed by *4.44* by Jay-Z as a response to *Lemonade*, and an apology, and then The Carters – their collaboration – rounds out the work with an album entitled *Everything is Love*. This is a clever instalment in a marriage machinery where there is misdirection and management devoted to gaining 'control of the narrative'[16] while also producing provocative popular culture. This commentary on marriage is creative as well as capitalist. Black people have been denied full entry into capitalism, their labour taken and redeployed in slavery and via entertainment industries. The popular music industry is rife with appropriations of black music by white musicians. The wisdom and awareness Beyoncé and Jay-Z display in how the entertainment industry operates to restrain and control black bodies, black art and black experiences is astute. Those that ask them to be beholden to a project of moral separation and resistive integrity misread the nuance with which the Carters navigate the dialogue between refusal and resistance. *Lemonade* is a launchpad for ambivalence – a smartly crafted product, but also an intervention into the personal as well as the political in tone and tunes. Its provocations around the (female) black body – how it is used, manipulated, changed and engaged – offers an interrogation of 'the real' as it is experienced by black women over time.

Colin Kaepernick also utilised his body as a cultural site as a black man in sport to prise open space for commentary. Kaepernick was considered one of the most talented and promising quarterbacks in the NFL until he failed to stand during the national anthem in 2016. After this protest, Kaepernick has been repeatedly blacklisted from games through injury or claims of poor performance. He has not started a game since and as of 2020 is unlikely to ever play in the NFL. His unruly black body mobilised a racialised refusal that could not be tolerated within the sporting industry that relies on compliance and a level of docility and performativity of the black male body for sporting consumers. This is affirmed in evidence that asserts the NFL as one of the most conservative sporting institutions in the United States.

> The N.F.L. and its 32 franchise owners, none of them African American, may be the most conservative fraternity of leaders in major American sports. They bathe their games in overtly patriotic ceremonies and discourage players, mostly hidden behind masks and uniforms or armour, from individual acts of showmanship. At least seven donated $1 million or more to Trump's inaugural committee, far more than any other sport's owners.[17]

This conservatism is why it was scandalous when Janet Jackson had a costume malfunction revealing her breast during the half-time show in 2004.[18] It was contrarily un-scandalous that Beyoncé in the half-time show of 2016 performed Formation (her first single from *Lemonade*) for the first time with herself and her dancers dressed in homage to the Black Panther movement. There are many answers to why Beyoncé's overt callback to the Panthers went largely unnoticed by the white mainstream but why Kaepernick's protest resulted in the collapse of his career and virtual banning from the sport. *Lemonade* is a fulcrum around which #BlackLivesMatter became mainstream and through which a deployment of black women's bodies and experiences is articulated and restrained. Kaepernick is a fulcrum around which refusal became visible. As long as resistance is entertaining it can be as rebellious as it wants. Capitalism colonises consciousness wherever it can. If that resistance slides over into refusal, it is problematic. This is why Beyoncé can perform Formation in homage to the Black Panthers but Kaepernick cannot take a knee. There is a slippery fluidity to the way black women's bodies enter entertainment, versus black male bodies, particularly in an era where black men are overly targeted by law enforcement for control. Unruliness is being brutally and publicly disciplined upon black (male) bodies. The docility of Kaepernick's protest was a potent refusal of violence in all forms. His docility was not submission. He was creating a chimera of blackness that defied and deified 'the real' experiences of black men.

Lemonade also drifts into the space of dreams and magic to display the dismay at being unable to intervene in 'the real', but also suggesting that dreams and magic are part of that real and present a radical alterity that transcends efforts to lock and curtail the range and type of debate that can be had in the public sphere about bodies, discipline, power, authority and community. The dreamlike qualities of the poetry and imagery convey the elemental nature of 'the real' being interrogated and the consequences for understanding in the everyday. The urgency of these narratives does not lose potency but shifts and changes in the struggle over meaning. When Colin Kaepernick dared to take a knee, the intensity of critique belied the subtlety of his protest. These distinctions collapse in 2020, when dreamy sequences and homages to magic morph into enragement at the sight of a public lynching of George Floyd by law enforcement, channelling Black Lives Matter into a hardened real of matter, solidity and tangibility that imagery condenses and cauterises.

The narrative around Kaepernick escalated quickly into a hypocritical confirmation of his right to protest but to not do it in that way. The national flag was codified as sacred and emphasis was placed on potential disrespect to service personnel. In the media, Kaepernick's 'protest was framed to be anti-military, antipolice and fundamentally anti-American, a direct contrast to the NFL's highly deliberate strategy of adopting American symbols and rituals'.[19] It is an irony unrivalled that these critiques covertly confirmed the para-militarisation of the police and that Kaepernick's protest against violence was counteracted by a discourse refusing to acknowledge the repressed truth of violence embedded in the American national narrative. Kaepernick's body had a requirement to compliance – he had a 'right' to protest but only within the accepted parameters of official authority. These were no more than pitiful, though powerful, attempts to reframe the terrain of debate by denying the legacy of Kaepernick's protest within the sit-ins of the civil rights era and co-opt an anti-national and anti-military discourse to diminish the context in which his protest was mobilised. When Megan Rapinoe demonstrated her support for Kaepernick by also taking a knee before 'a National Women's Soccer League match in Chicago in September 2016' it was similarly framed as selfish subversion of the comradery of team sports and an affront to national service personnel and the repressed truths of the wilful wielding of violence by those in power.[20]

Kaepernick's protest acknowledged that 'Black athlete activism transgressed the mainstream notion that professional sports was an egalitarian and meritorious space that provided a model for racial progress'.[21] He used sport to subvert the seduction of social mobility and enact an intervention via an educated hope. Kaepernick's consciousness was emergent out of his education. He drew upon the previous politics of Jackie Robinson 'who wrote weekly columns and books encouraging Black empowerment'[22] and Muhammad Ali who 'used the boxing ring and press conferences as spaces to contest racial hegemony'[23] and even the refusals of American Olympians Tommie Smith and John Carlos who 'defiantly raised their fists during a medal ceremony of the 1968 Olympics'. In harvesting this history Kaepernick was acknowledging the heritage of unequal access to power and the conduit of sport as a space in which to enact a refusal. By taking a knee, in demure deference and in physical docility, there sparked a violent reversal and reprisal because it was more than a peaceful protest, it was a double refusal. It was contrary to capitalism which is enfolded in the insistence of domination and the repressed truth of its violence. His interface of sport, popular culture and politics rewrote 'the real' for black bodies and channelled an educated hope in the moment of supplication that was transformed into commanding refusal.

Both the Lemonade Syllabus and the Colin Kaepernick Syllabus fuse high and low culture. By making popular culture worthy of public study rather than hidden away in degrees like media studies or cultural studies, these articulations of the popular as prescient situate the significance of educational literacies in semiotics and textual analysis to radical contemporary politics. The small gesture of taking a knee explodes into a complex history of bodies, power, race, athleticism and violence that requires elaborate literacies to grapple with. The fusion of rhythms, beats, lyrics, language, queer culture, southern identity, slavery, femininity and feminism, public and private spaces and the iconography of Beyoncé as a public woman in *Lemonade* renders performance and self into a composite relationship with 'the real' where a popular cultural site fuses and focuses these contexts.

These syllabi dance on the edges of the event. The evental potentiality of a black man taking a knee in protest at the football game or a radical fusion of feminism and funk in pop music bubbles insistently in the spaces of contested meaning. It is a radical thinking through of the everyday real in which popular culture interfaces with the self. It is a space within capitalism and consumption where a double refusal is possible. The perversions of popping the popular wherein radical feminism is commodified and black male bodies in sport are disciplined present the possibilities where capitalism does not close out consciousness. The possibilities of an educated hope mobilised in a hashtag syllabus that can filter through pop and open up spaces for thinking, processing, understanding and exploring is where the double refusal offers its greatest potential. This is not simply about making the personal political or the political personal, but understanding how constructs of race, class, gender, sexuality and age are crafted by external influences but play out in intimate spaces. Cultures of exploitation, oppression and dispossession infiltrate the norms of the everyday, and popular culture is often a site of mediation. 'The real' is beholden to the narratives that assert themselves on top of everyday sense-making but is resisted, rewritten or even refused in popular culture. It is no surprise that pop is a site of the most intensely commodified items, objects and ideas. The tenacity of such complexity needs containment by capitalism. The spaces for negotiation, re-reading, resistance and even refusal are pregnant with possibility. The evental erupts in double refusals.

NOTES

1. Sarah McPhee, "Coronavirus Australia: 'Make Your Way Home', PM Tells visa Holders," *news.com.au*, April 3, 2020, https://www.news.com.au/national/politics/coronavirus-australia-make-your-way-home-pm-tells-visa-holders/news-story/5568d4ef78610f1f7a06944916879693?fbclid=IwAR1bVH4B5hvpZLj3A7Na5CK9EeR7udi2BnV4_qERiDj1_YlXm8OdhJuMNf0.
2. Australian Government, Department of Education, *International Student Data: Monthly Summary*, February 2020, https://internationaleducation.gov.au/research/International-Student-Data/Documents/MONTHLY%20SUMMARIES/2020/Feb%202020%20MonthlyInfographic.pdf.
3. Hazel Ferguson and Henry Sherrell, "Overseas Students in Australian Higher Education" *Parliament of Australia*, June 20, 2019, https://www.aph.gov.au/About_Parliament/Parliamentary_Departments/Parliamentary_Library/pubs/rp/rp1819/Quick_Guides/OverseasStudents.
4. Adam Carey, Fergus Hunter, and Madeleine Heffernan, "Loss of International Students Set to Blow $30b-$60b Hole in Economy," *Sydney Morning Herald*, April 17, 2020, https://www.smh.com.au/politics/federal/loss-of-international-students-set-to-blow-30b-60b-hole-in-economy-20200416-p54kif.html.
5. Universities Australia, *The Facts on University Funding*, April 2017, https://www.universitiesaustralia.edu.au/wp-content/uploads/2019/05/University-Financing-Explainer-April-2017.pdf, 4.
6. James Doughney, "Without International Students, Australia's Universities Will Downsize – and Some Might Collapse Altogether," *The Conversation*, April 8, 2020, https://theconversation.com/without-international-students-australias-universities-will-downsize-and-some-might-collapse-altogether-132869.
7. Andrew Norton and Ittima Cherastidtham, *Mapping Australian Higher Education 2018*, Grattan Institute, Report No. 2018–11 September 2018, https://grattan.edu.au/wp-content/uploads/2018/09/907-Mapping-Australian-higher-education-2018.pdf, 37.
8. Paul Karp, "Australian Universities Warn Covid-19 Relief Package no Enough to Stop 21,000 Job Losses," *The Guardian*, April 12, 2020, https://www.theguardian.com/australia-news/2020/apr/12/australian-universities-warn-covid-19-relief-package-not-enough-to-stop-21000-jobs-losses.
9. Rana Foroohar, "Coronavirus Bursts the US College Education Bubble," *Financial Times*, April 26, 2020, https://www.ft.com/content/e5d50e86-861a-11ea-b872-8db45d5f6714?sharetype=blocked.

10. In 2014 it was reported in Graeme Turner and Kylie Brass *Mapping the Humanities, Arts and Social Sciences in Australia*, (Canberra: Australian Academy of the Humanities, 2014), 2 that the sector teaches 65% of Australia's students but "research income has fallen from 16% in 2014 to 13% by 2018." Khanh Tran, "The Slow Decline of Australian Humanities," *Honi Soit*, May 3, 2020, http://honisoit.com/2020/05/the-slow-decline-of-australian-humanities/. This is contrasted with the creation of specialist funding bodies for STEMM (Science, Technology, Mathematics and Medicine) dedicated to funnelling money to those disciplines, with the Medical Research Future Fund and the Defence Innovation Fund indicating "HASS does not have the same immediate access to government-funded research initiatives as STEM." Glenn Withers, John Beaton, Liz West, and Dylan Clements, *Funding for Social Science Research Pays its Way: The Response of the Academy of Social Sciences in Australia to the Standing Committee on Employment, Education and Training Inquiry into Funding Australia's Research*, June 29, 2018, (Canberra: Academy of the social sciences in Australia, 2018), 7. Furthermore, the research priorities of the ARC (Australia Research Council, the government research funding body) "focus on areas that appear to be the STEMM-driven, such as soil and water, cybersecurity, environmental change, and health." Rachel A. Ankeny and Lisa M. Given, "Creating Research Value Needs More Than Just Science – Arts, Humanities, Social Sciences Can Help," *The Conversation*, June 19, 2018, https://theconversation.com/creating-research-value-needs-more-than-just-science-arts-humanities-social-sciences-can-help-97083.
11. Candice Benbow, *Lemonade Syllabus*, accessed Jan 14, 2020, https://issuu.com/candicebenbow/docs/lemonade_syllabus_2016?e=24704410%2F35434012.
12. He had actually sat for two games previously, but he was "wearing street clothes while recovering from injuries" and so did not attract attention. Shane M. Graber, Ever J. Figueroa, and Krishnan Vasudevan, "Oh, Say, Can You Kneel: A Critical Discourse of Newspaper Coverage of Colin Kaepernick's Racial Protest," *Howard Journal of Communications*, 2019, doi: 10.1080/10646175.2019.1670295.
13. *The Colin Kaepernick Syllabus*, accessed January 23, 2020, https://docs.google.com/document/d/1RwDlBVRE_Yj_2l_a0EjAmukekUgxIrZfRVG0dEpJNOQ/mobilebasic.
14. Kyoko Shoji Hearn, "Violence, Storm, and the South in Beyoncé's Lemonade," *Lit: Literature Interpretation Theory* 30, no. 2, (2019): 156, https://doi.org/10.1080/10436928.2019.1597404.
15. Omise'eke Natasha Tinsley, "Beyoncé's Lemonade is Black Woman Magic," *Time*, April 25 2016, https://time.com/4306316/beyonce-lemonade-black-woman-magic/.
16. Constance Grady, "How Jay-Z and Beyoncé Use Music to Control the Narrative Around Their Marriage," *Vox*, June 17, 2018, https://www.vox.com/culture/2017/7/7/15914660/jay-z-beyonce-444-marriage.
17. John Branch, "The Awakening of Colin Kaepernick," *The New York Times*, September 7, 2017, https://www.nytimes.com/2017/09/07/sports/colin-kaepernick-nfl-protests.html.
18. It is also supposed to be rated PG13 for broadcast.

19. Danielle Sarver Coombes, Cheryl Ann Lambert, David Cassilo, and Zachary Humphries, "Flag on the Play: Colin Kaepernick and the Protest Paradigm," *Howard Journal of Communications*, (2019), https://doi.org/10.1080/10646175.2019.1567408, 8.
20. Coombes, Lambert, Cassilo, and Humphries, "Flag on the Play," 10.
21. Graber, Figueroa, and Vasudevan, "Oh, Say, Can You Kneel," 4.
22. Graber, Figueroa, and Vasudevan, "Oh, Say, Can You Kneel," 4.
23. Graber, Figueroa, and Vasudevan, "Oh, Say, Can You Kneel," 4.

INDEX

Ableism, 16–17, 112–113
Ableist gaze, 111–112
Abyssal thinking, 116–117
Accelerated capitalism, 12, 90–91
Accessibility, 115
Activism, 120
Against Our Will, 93
Ambivalence, 30
American Council on Education, 124
Andragogy, 67
Anna Lee Rain Yellowhammer, 73–74
Archive, 39, 40
Aspiration, 30
"Audacity of hope" rhetoric, 52–53

Barack Obama, 52
Baudrillard's maxim, 6
Beyoncé, 125
Bill Clinton, 52–53
Bismarck, 79–80
Black Panthers, 127
#BlackDisabledWomanSyllabus, 8, 113–115, 120
#BlackLivesMatter, 8, 50–52
Bodies, 7, 113–114
Brexit
  campaigners, 14–15
  decision, 42–43
Brutality, 18
Bursty dynamics, 3

Campus sanctuary movement, 104–105
Cannonball River, 73–74

Capitalism, 16–17, 28, 87–89, 90–91, 127
Catalogue, 40
Categorisation, 101–102
Center for Comparative Studies of Race and Ethnicity, The, 80
Charleston, 57–58
#CharlestonSyllabus, 57–58
#Charlottesville, 58
Cheyenne River Reservation, 73–74
Chronicle of Higher Education, The, 61
Chronicle Review, The, 61–62, 63
Citizenship, 104
Civic illiteracy, 63–64
Colin Kaepernick, 126–128
#ColinKaepernickSyllabus, 126–128
Commons-based peer production, 62
Commonwealth Grant Scheme (CGS), 123
Compassionate conservatism, 52–53
Consent, 7
Contemporary education, 33
Coronavirus crisis, 124
Council Lodge, 76
Critical Disability Studies, 113–114
Critical pedagogies, 6
Critical thinking, 2, 30–31
Crop-picking, 98

Crowd-sourced syllabus, 4–6, 44–46, 55, 56–57
  potency, 58
Crowd-sourcing, 44–45, 62–63
Culture of equivalence, 38
Curator, 38–40
Cynicism, 31–32

10 *Daily* story, 112–113
Dakota Access Pipeline (DAPL), 73–74
Decolonisation, 20
Deferred Action for Childhood Arrivals (DACA), 99–100, 104–105, 107
Deray McKesson, 54–55
Deviancy, 87–89
Digital economy, 62–63
Digitised communication, 81–82
Diminishment of expertise, 124
Disability, 113–114, 118–119
#Disabilitytoowhite, 113–115
Disabled body, 8
Disempowerment, 111–112
Disintermediation, 38
Docility, 126–127
Documentation, 101–102
Domination, 28
Donald Trump, 8, 14, 16, 42–43, 91–92, 99–100, 103
Double refusal, 1

Economics education, 11
Economy, 98
Educated hope, 5
Education, 1–2, 29, 33
  functions, 28
  middle-class tropes, 29–30
  within society, 12
Educational attainment, 27–28
Educators, 49–50
Electronic linking, 39. *See also* Hyperlinking
Elizabeth Heinman, 65–66
Emotional labour, 115–116
Endurance, 80–81

Energy Transfer Partners, 76
English Literature, 19
Equity, 40
European formations of citizenship, 101–102
Event, The, 6, 41–42
Everything is Love, 126
Exploitation, 28

Faith, 54–55
Fascism, 65
Federal Court of Appeals, 104
Feminism, 87–89, 129
Ferguson, 4–5, 7, 50–51, 57
#FergusonSyllabus, 7, 49–50, 50–51, 55, 57–58
French Revolution, 42

Gatekeepers, 41, 44–45
George Floyd, 127–128
Global 'post-content' hierarchy, 13–14
Global Financial Crisis, 11–14
Google, 37–38
GOP, 91–92

Hashtags, 3–4, 43–44
Henry Giroux, 63–64
Heritage, 39
Heterosexual pornography, 89
Heterosexuality, 90
History, 5, 18–19
Hope, 53–54, 57
Human rights, 8, 63–64
Hyperlinked online discourse, 34–35
Hyperlinking, 41

Ideal neoliberal citizen, 52–53
Illegals, 101
Illiteracy, 27
Immigration and Customs Enforcement (ICE), 98
Impairment, 113–114
Imperialist modernity, 20
Indigenous communities, 74–76
Indigenous knowledges, 77–79

Indigenous land rights, 74–75
Inspiration porn, 111–112
Intellectual disobedience, 2
Intellectual violence, 63–64

Jay-Z display, 126
Jean Baudrillard, 6

"Keep hope alive" slogan, 52–53
Knowledge, 1–2, 37–38
 free circulation of, 62

LaDonna Brave Bull Allard, 74
Lads, 25–29, 33
Land rights, 74–75
Language frames, 56
Learning, 68–69
Learning to Labour, 25–26
Learning to Labour in New Times, 30
Lemonade, 125–128
#LemonadeSyllabus, 125
Lexia, 39
Life-long learning, 33
Literacy, 37–38
 of expertise, 39

Male heterosexual sex, 87–89
Marcia Chatelain, 4–5, 7
Matthew Chrisler, 77
Meat-packing plants, 97–98
Medical model, 8
Memories, 40
#MeToo movement, 7, 86–87, 90–92
Michael Brown Jr., 50
Middle-class tropes of education, 29–30
Migrants, 101–102
Missouri River, 73–74
Mni Wiconi, 73–74
Modernity, 1, 18
Monetary management, 12

Naomi Klein, 74–75

National Vital Statistics System (NVSS), 51–52
Native title, 75–76
Neoliberal
 economisation, 12
 political systems, 13
 subject, 32–33
New School, 80
New York City Stands with Standing Rock Collective, 77
New York City University Sanctuary Coalition, 105
New York Times, The, 86
New York University (NYU), 105
#NewFascismSyllabus, 7, 65–71
NFL, 126–127
Nina-Marie Butler, 115–116
#NoDAPL, 73–74, 76–77
Non-US citizens, 106
#notallmen protest, 87
#NotOkay, 7, 90–94
NYU Sanctuary Coalition, 106–107

Oahe Dam, 73–74
Oceti Sakowin territory, 73–74
Official archives, 17–18
Ogallala aquifer, 80
Open-source, 62–63

PageRank
 algorithm, 38
 formula, 38
Paolo Freire, 113
Papereality, 101–102
Paranoia, 16–17
Paranoiac economy, 16–17
Patricia Cullors, 50
Paul Willis, 6, 25–26
Pedagogy of the Oppressed, 113
Peter McLaren, 5

Plyler v Doe, 104–105
Pornography, 89
Post-race, 51–52
Postcolonial world, 20
Predatory capitalism, 16–17
Provenance, 39
Pseudo-pacification process, 87–89
Public Books, 63–64

Radical thinking, 34–35
Ramp Your Voice, 113–114
Rape and Sexual Power in Early America, 92–93
Rape culture, 87, 90–91
#RapeCultureSyllabus, 85–87, 92–93
Records, 17
Refusal, 1, 107–108
Representation, 118–119
Repressed truth, 43–45
Resilience, 32–33
Resistance, 1
Rethinking, 3
Retweeting, 43
ReZpect Our Water movement, 73–74
Roman Empire, 17–18

Safety-valve, 102–103
Sanctuary, 102–103
   campus, 7–8
   cities and campuses, 100–101
   jurisdictions, 104
   syllabus, 107–108
Scott Morrison, 1
September 11 2001, 41
Sharing economy, 62
Silos, 19
Simon Winlow, 2
Simulacra, 87–89
Sit-in, 77–79
Social consciousness, 20
Social memory, 62–63
Social mobility, 6, 26, 29–30

Social model, 8, 41, 43, 50, 73, 76, 113–114
Standing Rock, 76–79
Standing Rock Reservation, 73–74
Standing Rock YouTube channel, 77–79
#StandingRockSyllabus, 7, 76–77, 79–82
Stella Young, 111–112
Steve Hall, 87–89
Stony Brook University, 80
Surf Lifesavers, 111

Takota Iron Eyes, 73–74
Teach-in, 77–79
Television networks, 97
Trump Syllabus, 61
   Trump1. 0 syllabus, 63
   Trump2. 0 syllabus, 63
Tweets, 43–44
Twin Towers, 42–43
Twitter
   functions, 43–44
   time, 44
   tools, 43
Twittersphere, 43–44

Ultra-realist refusal, 2–3
Unauthorized workers, 98
Unbiased reporting, 68–69
Uncivilised barbarians, 20
Undocumented sites, 97–98
Uniform Crime Report (UCR), 51–52
United Nations Declaration on the Rights of Indigenous Peoples, 75–76
Universities, 123
University of Manchester Post-Crash Economics Society, 11–12

Vilissa Thompson, 113–114, 119–120

Violence, 18, 90–91
Virtual labour market, 62

Walter Benjamin, 66–67
War and Warrior, 66–67
Water Protector, 73–74
Water rights, 75–76

Wilful ignorance, 128
Willis, 30–31
Working classes, 26, 30
   lads, 25

XOJane, 114

www.ingramcontent.com/pod-product-compliance
Lightning Source LLC
LaVergne TN
LVHW012249070526
838201LV00092B/168